CONGRESS AND
HIGHER EDUCATION
IN THE
NINETEENTH
CENTURY

·

CONGRESS AND HIGHER EDUCATION IN THE NINETEENTH CENTURY

GEORGE N. RAINSFORD

The University of Tennessee Press
Knoxville

Library of Congress Catalog Card Number 72–83343
International Standard Book Number 0–87049–140–7

To our children
Guy, Amy, Ann, Angela, and Emily,
and their generation,
whose education must be a matter
of consequence to all of us.

·

*The federal government has been a factor
in education for almost all of our national
history. But its role is changing—and
where the change is taking us no one can say.
No one knows how best to design the role
of the federal government in education. But
one thing is certain: with education playing
a vastly more crucial role in our national
life, there is no likelihood that the federal
government can escape greater involvement in it.*

—JOHN W. GARDNER

PREFACE

.

With the comment on the opposite page, John Gardner identified two major characteristics of the present status of federal assistance to education—greatly increased size of dollar involvement, and both change and uncertainty of future direction. From this identification naturally follow the questions, How did it all start and where is it going? The first question can be answered in some detail, as this book does, for it deals with the past. Moreover, an examination of the formative years of the history of federal assistance to higher education makes more clear the reasons for the composition and thrust of present programs. It also yields valuable clues in answering the question, Where is it all going?

In an interesting sense the wheel may have come full turn and it may be both necessary and desirable to move toward programs that appear to be new but in fact have origins in the nineteenth century or earlier. Current arguments for programs of institutional support as opposed to categorical grants, for support of public and private institutions alike, and for support of institutions generally in addition to support of students—all these have been tried in the past with differing success.

It is hard for anyone concerned with spiraling federal deficits and still unmet educational needs, both measured in terms of millions of dollars, to fail to be impressed with the size of current federal spending on higher education. In 1968–1969 that figure reached $3,228 million, an amount almost equivalent to the total generated by student fees.[1] This federal money

[1] American Council on Education, *A Fact Book on Higher Education* (Washington, D. C., 1971), p. 71.107.

vii

is not just the ivy on the walls of our colleges and universities. To a large degree it is the stone and mortar itself. Of the 2,600 institutions of higher education in 1969–1970, over 80 percent received some form of assistance from the federal government. Dozens of federal agencies supported hundreds of programs on as many campuses involving thousands of students, faculty members, administrators, or research personnel.

The financial pressures on our colleges and universities are well known. The gap between available income and normal expenses is widening. Institutions can affect some economies internally but even if their programs remain static, the costs will increase from 5 to 7 percent a year. Traditional public and private contributions are not likely to increase at that rate and because of a growing social-action orientation on the part of these benefactors, colleges and universities are pressured to become "agents of social change" in order to qualify for continued support. Finally, there is good reason not to shift a larger and larger burden onto the student at a time when college attendance is becoming a normal pattern for an increasing portion of our population. If this is indeed a national expectation, as indeed it appears to be, the federal government with its equitable and productive revenue system provides the logical and perhaps the only source to look to for significantly increased support. Such was the premise of the 1965 Federal Higher Education Act, the Miller bill in the Ninetieth Congress, and the House and Senate education bills in the Ninety-second Congress; the debates on these bills concerned only what level of increased support and what program contexts should be established.

Much has been written about federal aid to education and the subject has evoked considerable controversy. However, the enormous dollar values currently involved and the political nature of current discussions have tended to focus the emphasis of these writings on the contemporary scheme. Though the story of how and why present programs of federal spending came into being and how they fared is a fascinating one, interwoven with the lives of many famous Americans, it is a still neglected area of scholarship. As Bernard Bailyn, a Harvard historian, has written:

> Most of the important questions Americans are now asking about the development and impact of education remain unanswered by current historical writing. Despite the juxtaposition of historical curiosity and of devotion to education in the minds of many professional historians, few marriages of the two interests have taken place.[2]

The record of the past sometimes has been misinterpreted as well as ignored, to the detriment of our current understanding. For example, writers in the late nineteenth and early twentieth centuries, when the distinction between public and private education was a matter of much discussion, tended to read that distinction back into the colonial period where it had less validity. Land was the basis of the federal grants in the Ohio Contract of 1787 and the Morrill Act of 1862. Yet these two enactments of the national government served quite different purposes. Though they have been claimed as great milestones in the history of the government's support of higher education, it can be argued that assistance to education was simply of incidental importance to their enactors. The same can be said of the 1957 National Defense Education Act, about which Robert M. Hutchins remarked:

> History will smile sardonically at the spectacle of this great country getting interested slightly and temporarily in education only because of the technical advancements of Russia, and then being able to act as a nation only by assimilating education into a cold war and calling an education bill a defense act.[3]

Historians would be less apt to "smile sardonically" at the situation described by Mr. Hutchins if they were more familiar with the history of government support of American education

[2] Bernard Bailyn, *Education in the Forming of American Society* (Chapel Hill, 1960), x.
[3] Robert Hutchins, quoted in F. J. Seidner, *Federal Support for Education* (Washington, D. C., 1959), 1.

ix

as it developed over the last four hundred years. Likewise, people interested in understanding the nature of present problems in federal aid to education would do well to understand its history.

It is encouraging that American historians and educators have begun to research and publish in the field, thereby adding the dimension of historical insight to current discussions of educational policy.[4] My effort has been to add to this literature by examining that aspect of the public record of the nineteenth century most likely to cast light on the size and complexity of federal programs of assistance to higher education in the twentieth century.

Encouragement to do this work came from colleagues on the faculties of History and Education at Stanford University. Without the enthusiastic support and generous criticism of Donald Fehrenbacher, George Knowles, and W. H. Cowley, my interest in this area would never have come to its present fruition. The time necessary for scholarship was carved out of busy administrative and teaching careers with the aid of colleagues at the University of Denver and the University of Colorado. Invaluable secretarial help came from the staff of the President's office at the University of Colorado. Finally, my wife, Jean, and our five children uncomplainingly shared husband and father with his work in such a supportive and enthusiastic way as to make me feel that I was doing something for all of them. All of this simply proves that the production of a book is a joint venture in which all concerned justly share the credit because they have shared the work involved.

GEORGE N. RAINSFORD

Kalamazoo, Michigan
February, 1972

[4] Lawrence A. Cremin, "The Recent Development of the History of Education as a Field of Study in the United States," *History of Education Journal* 7 (1955–1956):1–35.

CONTENTS

.

CONGRESS AND
HIGHER EDUCATION
IN THE
NINETEENTH
CENTURY

.

1. COLONIAL BACKGROUNDS

.

Government support of higher education, in the American experience, began during the colonial period. The roots of today's programs of aid, at all educational levels and from a variety of governmental sources, reach back to the practices of royal governors, legislation of colonial assemblies, and acts of the Crown. An entirely different environment for government support of education existed in the colonial era, however, and the contemporary assistance to public education from tax dollars is more than a mere three-hundred-year extension of the pioneering Massachusetts School Law of 1647.[1]

More than in the twentieth century, society in the sixteenth and seventeenth centuries was hierarchical in both theory and practice. Government represented not the whole body of society but rather a political, religious, social, and financial oligarchy bulwarked by church and state. Justification for education rested on design for leadership, not citizenship, and served primarily the interest of making good Christians rather than good citizens.

New Englanders equated savagery and barbarism with illiteracy, and because of this the leaders of society thought it their particular duty to establish schools and colleges and to support education.[2] Thus an act of the General Court of Massachusetts Bay in 1642 made compulsory the attainment of the level of education necessary "to read & understand the

---

[1] Bailyn, 14.
[2] George Lee Haskins, *Law and Authority in Early Massachusetts* (New York, 1960), 66–84 and chs. 3–5 generally.

principles of religion & the capitall lawes of this country. . . ."[3] The 1647 act of this same body legislated the nation's first public support for local schools. A century later, general instructions to the royal governors in 1758 urged that recommendations be made to the assemblies "to enter upon proper methods for the erecting and maintaining of schools in order to the training up of youth to reading and to a necessary knowledge of the principles of religion."[4]

Although private benefaction and private responsibility remained at the foundation of education, other colonial governments followed Massachusetts's lead and encouraged the establishment of schools and colleges, granting most of the institutions founded some form of public aid. Government support did not provide completely for the annual expense of any of these early educational institutions, but without some such assistance few of them could have survived. Most education exhibited a mixed nature, being private in its organization though semipublic in its financing. Thus the distinction between public and private education, so pronounced in current discussions of federal aid to higher education, had as little meaning in the colonial context as did the idea of separation between church and state. In fact, in this regard colonial America more closely resembled sixteenth- and seventeenth-century England than it did nineteenth- and twentieth-century America. Government support of education represented as much the extension of an English practice as it did the beginning of an American one. Interaction with the colonial environment changed the original English pattern, but the English origins are clear.

Landholdings figured prominently in the development of the great centers of higher education in western Europe, which were closely associated with religious establishments. Educa-

[3] Nathaniel B. Shurtleff, ed., *Records of the Governor and Company of the Massachusetts Bay in New England, 1628–1686* (Boston, 1853), 2:6.

[4] Leonard W. Labaree, ed., *Royal Instructions to British Colonial Governors, 1670–1776* (New York, 1935), 2:504.

tion served the interest of the religious hierarchy and received support in turn from the substantial income which these establishments possessed by virtue of their great landholdings.

In sixteenth-century England, following the final dissolution of the monasteries under Henry VIII and Edward VI, many educational centers lost this financial support. Fees from students proved then insufficient to maintain schools and colleges, which had seldom been self-supporting. The crisis came for Oxford and Cambridge when courtiers began to cast longing eyes on the land endowments of these colleges, which remained Catholic at heart. In 1544, Parliament passed "An Act for the Dissolution of the colleges"; and in 1545, Henry VIII established a royal commission to report on their revenues and expenditures. The findings showed that these institutions were frequently "embarrassed by the insufficiency of their revenues to meet their ordinary expenses," which caused Henry to declare that he "thought he had not in his realme so many persons so honestly maynteyned in lyvying bi so little land and rent."[5]

Henry preserved the college charters and announced his desire rather to advance learning and "erecte new occasion thereof, than to confound those your ancyent and godly instytutions."[6] He designated a significant part of the expropriated religious land as new endowment for schools and colleges. A royal gift of land provided endowment for two new colleges at each Oxford and Cambridge as well as income for five Regius Professorships. The action of the king established a practice followed by others, and land owned by educational institutions in England soon became an important element in their financing.

Gifts of land or rents likewise constituted important items in the first efforts of the English settlers to establish a college in the American colonies. Regular grants from tax revenues had not been part of the English experience and "the English

---

[5] James Bass Mullinger, *The University of Cambridge* (Cambridge, England, 1884), 2:79.
[6] Ibid., 80.

who settled Virginia and New England were unused to supporting education out of taxation. Their schools and university colleges were maintained by endowments largely in the form of land that yielded rent."[7] In the colonies, the eventual broadening of government support to include grants from tax revenues thus illustrates one of the important results of the interaction of English usage with colonial environment.

In the English economy, the concentration of land ownership resulting from the operation of the feudal system meant that tenancy constituted the normal type of land occupancy. This fact insured a reliable source of income in the form of rent produced from the land, since, if one tenant proved unsatisfactory, others could be found to take his place. Parliament, however, realizing that land rents did not always reflect the conditions of the rising price of land, in 1575 passed an act which provided that one-third of the rents from university land endowments could be paid in "corn and malt at a fixed price of that date."[8] As the price of corn and malt rose steadily, universities with land endowment could receive one-third of their income in commodities that constantly increased in value.[9]

Differences in the colonial environment made it impossible to duplicate English practices. In the colonial society of unlimited land, limited population, and a widely fluctuating economy, land rents gave no assurance of secure income over a period of time. Untenanted land, moreover, promised only future profits and could not provide for current expenses. Finally, private contributions proved inadequate and unreliable.

The first experiment with higher education in English-speaking America demonstrated the problem of operating a college with income solely derived from land endowment and gifts. Henrico College, chartered in 1619 by the Crown, re-

[7] Samuel E. Morison, "The History of Universities," *Rice Institute Pamphlets*, 23, no. 4 (Oct. 1936), 271.

[8] Lionel Lancelot Shadwell, ed., *Enactments in Parliament Concerning Oxford and Cambridge* (Oxford, 1912), 1:190.

[9] Wallace Notestein, *The English People on the Eve of Colonization, 1603–1630* (New York, 1954), 131.

ceived a grant of 10,000 acres from the Virginia Company as its principal means of support. The Crown encouraged the enterprise since founding of the college had as its main purpose to "bring the infidels and savages, living in those parts, to human civility, and to a settled and quiet government. . . ."[10]

With the support of the king, and with the aid of the established church, the company collected a general capital contribution in England for the college, recruited tenants, and shipped them to the colony. The company also sent a minister to have supervision of the tenants and gave him five acres and a yearly salary of £40.[11] The tenants, however, produced few crops, were maintained only at great cost, and left the land either to farm for themselves or to work for other planters at the first opportunity. Finally, an Indian massacre and the revocation of the company's charter ended an experiment which had proved marginal from its inception.[12]

When private benefactions and land endowments alone proved insufficient to maintain a college in the colonial environment, the colonists realized they required regular government assistance and many means were tried. These included donations of receipts from certain taxes; licenses; and lotteries; referral of income from public utilities, such as mills and ferries; and grants of patronage fees.[13] It became clear, however, that only direct and repeated contributions from the community in the form of voluntary donations and taxation could provide adequate means of support. The colonial experience, then, came to differ substantially from the English in that many educational enterprises received regular government support. An examination of the history of the founding of the colonial colleges will illustrate the many practices involved.

The General Court of Massachusetts assisted Harvard Col-

[10] Robert H. Land, "Henrico and Its College," *William and Mary Quarterly*, 2nd ser. 18 (1938):470.

[11] Ibid., 479.

[12] W. H. Cowley, "A Short History of American Higher Education" (unpublished MS, Stanford University, 1961), 3, 6.

[13] Elsie W. Clews, *Educational Legislation and Administration of the Colonial Governments* (New York, 1899), 501.

lege from the time of its chartering in 1636. On October 28, 1636, it agreed "to give 400 £ towards a schoale or colledge, whereof 200 £ to bee paid the next yeare, & 200 £ when the worke is finished, & the next Court to appoint wheare & wt building."[14] This amount constituted a substantial sum for so small a community, as it represented more than one-half the entire tax levy for the colony for 1635 and almost one-quarter of the levy for 1636. In 1640, Harvard received a grant of the ferry tolls between Boston and Charlestown and an annual rate of £100 for general support. The General Court paid the college president's salary for several years and provided for the costs of buildings and repairs. It sponsored lotteries on behalf of the college, and it levied a tax of one peck of corn or its value equivalent from each family for a time in the middle of the seventeenth century. Moreover, students and officers received exemption from military service and taxation.[15]

In 1701 the General Court of Connecticut endowed "the Collegiate School of Connecticut" (later Yale) with a charter and an annual grant of £120 current money or the equivalent of £60 sterling.[16] The General Court had as its announced motive that "Youth may be instructed in the Arts and Sciences who through the blessing of almighty God may be fitted for Publick employment both in Church & Civil State." In 1703 it freed the students from military service and the payment of taxes. But local jealousies retarded the success of the school

[14] Shurtleff, *Records of Massachusetts*, I, 183.

[15] Margery S. Foster, *"Out of Smalle Beginings . . ."* An Economic History of Harvard College in the Puritan Period, 1636–1712 (Cambridge, Mass., 1962), 85–105. This book contains a detailed record of the grants made to the college and the money received. It is clear from reading the record that not all the grants made were received in their entirety due to a lack of cash. This was even true of the founding grant of £400. This finding with regard to the relations between the General Court and Harvard College in Massachusetts is also borne out in studies of other colonial colleges and their respective colonial governments.

[16] *Acts of the General Assembly of Connecticut with Other Permanent Documents Respecting Yale University* (New Haven, 1901), 6.

by postponing the fixing of a permanent site and consequently discouraging major private donations. The General Court made a grant of 250 acres, and when New Haven offered an endowment of £700, the location became settled. In response to repeated memorials of the trustees, the school received additional legislative grants of money and deeds of land. A tax of fourpence per gallon of rum imported into the colony was levied for several years to aid in the building of the rector's house.[17]

On February 8, 1693, the joint sovereigns, William and Mary, granted a royal charter to the college in Virginia which still bears their names. The charter contained the following provision for a grant of 20,000 acres: "Ten thousand Acres of Land, not yet legally occupied or possessed by any of our other Subjects, lying, and being on the south side of the Blackwater Swamp; and also other ten thousand Acres of Land . . . [at] Pamunkey Neck."[18]

Because of the prior experience with Henrico, however, the royal couple also provided grants of £1,958 14s. 10d.; the revenue from a duty of a penny a pound on all tobacco exported from one English plantation in America to another; and the power to appoint the surveyor general of the colony and use the fees of his office. The college also received the right to nominate one person to the House of Burgesses in order to insure continual good relations with the provincial government.

The early history of these three colleges founded in the seventeenth and early eighteenth centuries illustrates the wide range of methods used by colonial governments in support of education. Each college received a grant of land at its founding and frequent legislative and executive subventions. The

[17] Franklin B. Dexter, ed., *Documentary History of Yale University, 1701–1745* (New Haven, 1916), 22, 207, 221.

[18] Henry Hartwell, James Blair, Edward Chilton, eds., *The Present State of Virginia and the College* (written 1697 in Virginia, published 1727 in London, reprinted in present edition, Williamsburg, Va., 1940), 92.

high level of support of education in New England reflected the presence of established churches, the existence of self-governing colonies whose political and religious leadership were the same, and the convenience of a township pattern of local government and land development. Royal support for the College of William and Mary reflected the interests of the Crown in assisting an enterprise of the Church of England. In the other middle and southern colonies, less unity between government and church, and the lack of a centralized form of local government, meant that not only higher but also secondary and elementary education developed more slowly.

For colleges founded after the middle of the eighteenth century, government support became harder to obtain. The Great Awakening stimulated religious diversity and made it difficult for any denominational group to secure assistance from an Anglican governor or an assembly representing a different sectarian persuasion. Government support for higher education became more indirect, taking the form of sponsored lotteries, licensed fund-raising drives, and the granting of charters with broad powers. As a result, by the time of the Revolution, all the newer colleges, except King's in New York, operated at a deficit.[19]

Emerging ideas of separation of church and state and the beginning of more broadly based political structures raised questions about governmental support of church-dominated education. The Anglican royal governors and the Assembly of New Jersey maintained a friendly attitude toward education, but they did not grant financial aid to either the College of New Jersey (Presbyterian) or Queen's College (Dutch Reform). Funds had to be raised privately in both cases before the Crown granted charters to the College of New Jersey in 1746 and to Queen's College in 1766. The College of New Jersey settled in Princeton only because the town came forward

[19] Beverly McAnear, "College Founding in the American Colonies, 1745–1775," *Mississippi Valley Historical Review* 42 (1955–1956): 40.

with a gift of £1,000 plus ten acres for a campus and 200 acres of woodlands for fuel.[20]

The University of Pennsylvania, founded first as Franklin's Academy in 1749, received support from the city of Philadelphia because of its combination with a charitable school and because of its interdenominational nature. When the proprietors granted a college charter in 1753, the Common Council of the city granted £200 with a promise of an annual endowment of £100 for five years. The mayor also granted £100 out of his own salary in lieu of the usual "mayor's entertainment."[21] The college also profited from the state's policy of favoring charitable institutions by granting them lottery privileges. But when the proprietors appointed an Anglican as provost, the Quakers and German sectarians who dominated the Assembly responded by passing legislation suppressing lotteries.[22]

King's College (Columbia), located in a royal colony and largely supported by Anglicans, enjoyed a more prosperous existence than other colleges located in colonies divided by religious differences. At the request of the Assembly and the Council in 1746, the governor began licensing lotteries for the support of a college. The language of the public bills authorizing these lotteries indicated than any member who voted to use the money raised for any other purpose would be declared forever incapable of sitting or voting in the Assembly.[23]

The colony raised sufficient funds so that by 1751 the governor created a board of trustees, and in 1754 the Crown granted a charter. The king gave £400 to the venture, the Assembly having already voted £500 annually for seven years from money raised by the excise tax.[24] The college then re-

[20] George P. Schmidt, *Princeton and Rutgers* (Princeton, 1964), 4.
[21] Edward Potts Cheyney, *History of the University of Pennsylvania, 1740–1940* (Philadelphia, 1940), 36.
[22] Clews, *Educational Legislation*, 308–10.
[23] Ibid., 249.
[24] *A History of Columbia University, 1754–1904* (New York, 1904), 4.

ceived a large tract of land from Trinity Church in New York through the efforts of the bishop of London, a trustee. Between 1754 and the Revolution, the governor committed over 35,000 acres to the use of the college, all of which land was later lost in a boundary dispute between New York and New Hampshire.

The College of Rhode Island (Brown) began in 1764 "without funds, without students, and with no present prospect of support. . . ."[25] The Assembly granted no financial aid because the Baptist control of the college promoted sectarian bickerings, but the charter exempted students and faculty from taxation, jury duty, and military service.[26]

Dartmouth, the last of the colonial colleges founded before the Revolution, received its royal charter in 1769. A group of New Hampshire Congregational ministers had been refused a college charter in 1758 by Benning Wentworth, the Anglican governor. Eleazar Wheelock, meanwhile, had established a school in Connecticut to Christianize the Indians. Lord Dartmouth, a trustee, then headed a fund drive in England for the school which netted over £9,000, the largest sum raised to that time by an American college. The missionary nature of the school attracted wide support.[27]

The school received a grant in 1761 of £72 a year from the Massachusetts legislature to pay for the education of six Indian students. In 1762 the New Hampshire legislature granted £50 a year for five years for general support. Seeing Wheelock's success, the Congregational ministers abandoned their separate efforts to found a New Hampshire college and joined the new governor, John Wentworth, in attempting to secure

[25] Reuben A. Guild, "The First Commencement of Rhode Island College," *Collections of the Rhode Island Historical Society* 7 (1885): 270.

[26] John Russell Bartlett, ed., *Records of the Colony of Rhode Island and Providence Plantations, in New England* 6 (Providence, 1861): 385–91.

[27] Leon B. Richardson, *History of Dartmouth College* (Hanover, N. H., 1932), 1:56, 86, 88.

a New Hampshire site for the Connecticut Indian school. Through the efforts of Wentworth, the Crown issued a charter in 1769 and granted a large tract of land in Hanover. Wentworth also assisted in securing a grant of £500 from the Assembly in 1773.[28]

Well-established precedent for government support of college education existed by the end of the colonial period. Where religious unity characterized the society of a colony, education received more extensive support than where denominational conflict existed. Yet religious differences were largely submerged in the political atmosphere surrounding the Revolution, and by the end of the colonial period, political and constitutional issues had replaced those involving religion. As colonial assemblies acquired more political power, it became increasingly important to secure their favor before financial aid could be obtained. The granting of property rights in the income from government offices, as in the case of the College of William and Mary, declined as government became more representative of all the groups in society and the assemblies came to reflect local and increasingly democratic interests. Moreover, local assistance in the form of land grants for site locations and other sources of local revenue evidenced the growing importance of local support and control. This trend blossomed subsequently in states' rights notions about education.

The resources available to government in its efforts to support education reflected the nature of government as well as of the economy. As a consequence of the change in the nature and function of government, proprietary rights in government offices and in public utility services could no longer be granted as gifts of income, and the distinction between public and private funds came to have real meaning. The choice of resources, the educational programs to which they would be

---

[28] Nathaniel Bouton, ed., *Provincial papers. Documents and records relating to the province of New Hampshire, from the earliest period of its settlement: 1623–[1776]* 7 (Nashua, N. H., 1873):323.

applied, and the manner of their application were all matters that had to be worked out before the new nation could develop a program of government support of education. But, the patterns which emerged and which are the subject of this book had their roots in the colonial period.

2. A NATIONAL UNIVERSITY,

THE CONSTITUTION,

AND PUBLIC POLICY

.

The colonial period left a legacy of government interest in higher education which did not dissipate even during the Revolution. The first nationally sponsored educational program, in fact, began while the country was at war and involved "general instruction" (principally in mathematics) of men in the Continental Army under the Von Steuben Regulations of 1779.[1] State governments did not lag behind. The 1776 constitutions of Pennsylvania and North Carolina pledged support of "seminaries of learning" (meaning colleges and universities). In 1777 the Vermont constitution stated that "one grammar school in each county, and one university in this State, ought to be established by direction of the General Assembly."[2]

In the history of public education, changes in the pattern and function of education have frequently been brought about

---

[1] The educational activities of the Congress during the Confederation period which culminated in the Land Ordinance of 1785 and the Northwest Ordinance and Ohio Company Contract of 1787 are discussed in ch. 3.

[2] The state of Vermont was originally claimed by Massachusetts, New Hampshire, and New York, and at the commencement of the revolutionary struggle she not only sought independence from British rule but from the states of New York and New Hampshire. These matters were not finally settled until 1790, when New York consented to the admission of Vermont into the Union. The constitution, however, was framed in 1777 and although not taken to the people for ratification, it was affirmed by the legislature at its sessions in 1779 and 1782 and declared to be a part of the laws of the state. U. S., Congress, House, *House Document* 357, 59 Cong., 2 sess., 6:3737 (cumulative *House Documents*, vol. 91, pt. 2).

by the changes in the philosophy of government. Because the American government today is democratic and popular, public education is concerned principally with equalizing opportunity and creating minimum standards. It is primarily directed to the strengthening of mass education so that the benefits of education may be spread more widely. In the colonial period education served a different and narrower purpose, being directed more specifically to satisfying, at the college level, the needs of political and religious leadership.

During the revolutionary period the political basis of government, and therefore the function of education, began to change. The federal and some new state constitutions provided for the separation of church and state. Thus politics became less the prerogative of religious leadership and more the concern of all citizens who had now to be educated to their new responsibilities.

After the achievement of independence, when the urge to create new symbols of nationalism and national culture ran high, the debate continued over the proper extent and nature of the central government's participation in, and support of, higher education. Debate over the character of federal-state relations in education was concerned with the more general question of the locus of sovereignty. To what extent should the educational system of the nation be state-oriented or national? Could the federal government support national institutions and programs directly, or should it channel its support through the state governments and be directed to the support of local institutions and programs?

In this debate, supporters of the new French liberalism as well as of American nationalism suggested creating a clearly national system of education supported and controlled by the central government.[3] The idea of a national system, however, ran counter to two strong currents. Even though some leaders made efforts to secularize education, it remained closely

[3] Allen O. Hansen, *Liberalism and American Education in the Eighteenth Century* (New York, 1926). This work contains excerpts from many of the proposed plans for a national system of education.

associated with religion. In the absence of a nationally established church (as in France and England), the obvious question arose as to which church or churches would control the proposed national system. Further, the aggressive local, states' rights attitude exhibited in the Continental and Confederation congresses made it clear that for constitutional as well as educational reasons, many people continued to think of education as a local matter.

A proposed compromise suggested that states, local communities, and private groups continue to exercise primary responsibility for education, and that the federal government cap the system with a national university. As a United States commissioner of education much later remarked, "national education does not begin as is sometimes supposed, with primary education, but with higher education."[4]

At the Constitutional Convention of 1787, Charles Pinckney of South Carolina submitted his plan of government which authorized Congress "to establish and provide for a national university at the seat of government of the United States."[5] Pinckney further moved to give Congress the power "to establish seminaries for the promotion of literature, and the arts and sciences." James Madison also held that Congress could "establish an university."

Nothing came of these proposals, and on September 14, 1787, shortly before the final adjournment of the convention, Madison and Pinckney again moved that Congress be empowered "to establish a university, in which no preferences or distinctions should be allowed on account of religion."[6] The motion for even this rather limited action failed 6 to 4 in spite of the fact that the university was now designated as federal, not national. Gouverneur Morris of Pennsylvania, among the

---

[4] W. T. Harris, Oct. 1, 1891, quoted in George Gary Bush, *History of Higher Education in Massachusetts* (Washington, D. C., 1891), 3.

[5] Jonathan Elliot, ed., *Debates on the Adoption of the Federal Constitution, in the Convention held in Philadelphia in 1787* 5 (Washington, D. C., 1845): 130.

[6] Ibid., 544.

opponents of the measure, observed, "It is not necessary. The exclusive power at the seat of government will reach the object."

From the limited coverage of the debate in the official records of the convention or in presidential papers, it is difficult to establish the grounds for the action taken. In any case, the Constitution as adopted and ratified contained no reference to support of education by the federal government. In fact, the word *education* appears nowhere in the document.[7]

This omission did not deter President Washington from urging Congress to consider the matter. In his first message to Congress, January 8, 1790, he extolled the virtues of knowledge as the surest basis of public happiness and as particularly essential in a republic. After describing the potential contributions of education to the proper ordering of the new nation, he concluded: "Whether this desirable object will be best promoted by affording aids to seminaries already established, by the institution of a national university, or by any other expedients, will be well worthy of a place in the deliberations of the Legislature."[8]

This portion of Washington's address came before the House of Representatives for consideration on May 3, 1791. A Maryland delegate, Michael Stone, asked "what part of the Constitution authorized Congress to take any steps in a business of this kind." He observed that Congress had already encouraged learning in protecting authors through the recently passed copyright law, and he added, "this is going as far as we have the power to go by the Constitution." Roger Sherman of Connecticut recalled that an authorization of authority had been proposed and "negatived" in the convention. "It was

---

[7] Even ART. 1, SEC. 8, which provided the congressional power for "organizing, arming, and disciplining the Militia," specifically reserved to the states "the Authority of training the Militia according to the discipline prescribed by Congress. . . ."

[8] U. S., Congress, *Annals of the Congress of the United States: The Debates and Proceedings in the Congress of the United States, 1789–1824*, 1 Cong., 2 sess., vol. 1, p. 934.

thought sufficient that this power should be exercised by the States in their separate capacity."[9] John Page of Virginia, in attempting to resolve the issue,

> observed that he was in favor of the motion [to refer the President's speech to a special committee]. He wished to have the matter determined, whether Congress has, or has not, a right to do anything for the promotion of science and literature. He rather supposed that they had such a right; but if, on investigation of the subject, it shall appear they have not, he should consider the circumstances as a very essential defect in the Constitution, and should be for proposing an amendment; for, on the diffusion of knowledge and literature, depend the liberties of this country, and the preservation of the Constitution.[10]

At any rate, Alexander Hamilton of New York articulated the Federalist broad-construction view of the constitutional power of Congress when, in his 1791 report on manufactures, he said, "There seems no doubt that whatever concerns the general interests of learning and agriculture, manufactures and commerce, are within the sphere of the national council so far as regards the application of money."

Washington used his executive authority to set aside land in the capital city as a site for the national university in the evident hope that Congress would act or that private contributions would be raised to found the institution. Yet Congress refused to act even on the limited basis of establishing a corporation to receive private donations in support of the president's plan. In the debate on the matter, the following arguments appeared among the objections raised: there was no constitutional authority for such a move; the institution should be called "An University of the District of Columbia" and not "a national university," which was something "materially different"; the institution would be a financial burden on the nation, requiring funds for its support from the general revenues. Washington's hopes for a national university could

[9] Ibid., vol. 2, p. 1551.
[10] Ibid.

not be dissipated, however, and he left his country a gift in his will to be used as endowment for the university when established.

In several of his messages to Congress, Washington also urged the creation of a military academy. There was almost no congressional debate on the constitutional basis of the military academy, though it also served as a limited kind of educational institution. Since the academy did not plan to offer a full collegiate degree program for many years, established colleges did not fear competition. Since only the federal government could maintain an army, no federal-state issue arose. The constitutional justification seemed to have been that of providing for the "common defense." The "Act fixing the Military Peace Establishment of the United States," which created the Academy at West Point, passed on March 16, 1802.[11] The principal debate occasioned by this bill was on the size of the corps to be stationed there, not on the question of the federal government's authority to establish an educational institution.

Each of the first six presidents urged Congress to take some action to establish a national university, although Jefferson and Monroe both thought it necessary first to amend the Constitution. In his second annual message, on December 5, 1810, Madison proposed the establishment of a national university in such a way as to weaken objections. It was to have the character

> of superadding to the means of education, provided by the several States, a seminary of learning, instituted by the National Legislature, within the limits of their exclusive jurisdiction, the expense of which might be defrayed or reimbursed out of the vacant grounds which have accrued to the nation within those limits.

> Such an institution, though local in its legal character, would be universal in its beneficial effects.[12]

[11] Ibid., 7 Cong., 1 sess., 1306–12.
[12] Ibid., 11 Cong., 3 sess., 13.

The select committee, appointed by the House of Representatives to examine this recommendation of the president, fully discussed the constitutional and policy questions involved. The report recognized the importance of the institution proposed. It also accepted the concept that although the Constitution did not specifically warrant the creation of such a university, Congress had the power to establish a university in the federal capital under the grant of exclusive jurisdiction at the seat of government. Beyond this point the report remained essentially negative:

> Here, however, other considerations arise. Although there is no Constitutional impediment to the incorporation of trustees for such a purpose, at the City of Washington, serious doubts are entertained as to the right to appropriate the public property for its support. The endowment of the university is not ranked among the objects for which drafts ought to be made upon the Treasury. The money of the nation seems to be reserved for other uses.
>
> The matter then stands thus: The erection of a university, upon the enlarged and magnificent plan which would become the nation, is not within the power confined by the Constitution to Congress; and the erection of a small and ordinary college, with a pompous and imposing title, would not become its dignity. If, nevertheless, at any time legislative aid should be asked to incorporate a district university, for the local benefit of the inhabitants of Columbia, and of funds of their own raising, there can be no doubt that it would be considered with kindness, as in other cases; but it must be remembered that this is a function totally distinct from the endowment of a national university, out of the treasure of the United States, destined, in its legislative application, to other and very different purposes.[13]

Interest in a national university took a new turn during the presidential terms of James Monroe and John Quincy Adams. In 1821, Congress granted a corporate charter to "The Columbia College" under its local legislative power for

---

[13] Ibid., 976–77.

the District of Columbia.[14] Monroe hoped that this institution would fulfil the functions which had so often been ascribed to the proposed national university. To further this purpose, in 1825, Congress donated building lots in the District to the college valued at $25,000.[15] It is important to note, as some authorities have failed to do, that the donation was of land and not of money. This gift thus involved no new principle since all agreed that Congress had constitutional power to dispose of land within the District of Columbia in any way it deemed appropriate.

The founding of the Columbia College failed to satisfy those ambitious for a national university, and interest in the proposed institution revived when the United States government became the residual legatee of James L. Smithson, the illegitimate son of the Duke of Northumberland. In his will, Smithson left property valued at over $500,000 which, after the fulfilment of certain conditions, became in 1836 the property of the United States. The stipulated use was "to found at Washington, under the name of The Smithsonian Institution, an establishment for the increase and diffusion of knowledge among men." The story of the development of the Smithsonian Institution is not of concern here. It suffices to observe that from the start it seemed fairly clear that the Smithson bequest would not be used to create either a college or a university.[16] All the arguments used both for and against a national university, however, were applied to the proposed new institution and the relationship of Congress to it. This fact delayed its establishment as a museum and research institution until 1846.

The growing sectionalism leading up to the outbreak of the Civil War precluded consideration of any institution that

[14] By act of Congress, June 23, 1904, the name of the institution was changed to "The George Washington University."

[15] U. S., Congress, *Congressional Debates: Register of Debates in Congress, 1824–1837*, 22 Cong., 1 sess., vol. 8, pt. 2:3210.

[16] David Madsen, *The National University—Enduring Dream of the U. S.* (Detroit, 1966), 61.

could be described as "national." The resurgence of national-ism during and following the war made possible the presenta-tion in Congress of two national university bills. The first of these, submitted by Senator Frederick A. Sawyer of South Carolina in 1872, represented the views of the recently or-ganized National Education Association. It proposed a na-tional university endowed with federal donations of $20 million in United States certificates bearing 5 percent interest. The second bill, submitted by Senator Timothy O. Howe of Wisconsin, closely resembled the first.

The following year, possibly reacting to the reform pres-sures of 1872, President Grant took up the cause of a national university. His December 2, 1873, message to Congress in-cluded this passage: "I would suggest to Congress the pro-priety of promoting the establishment in this District of an institution of learning, or university, of the highest class by donation of lands. There is no place better suited for such an institution than the national capital. There is no other place in which every citizen is so directly interested."[17]

President Hayes also supported the idea of a national uni-versity but more as a capstone to the public school system of the District of Columbia. In 1878 he asserted:

The wisdom of legislation upon the part of Congress in
aid of the States for education of the whole people in those
branches of study which are taught in the common schools
of the country is no longer a question. The intelligent judge-
ment of the country goes still further, regarding it as also
both constitutional and expedient for the General Government to extend to technical and higher education such aid as
is deemed essential to the general welfare . . . .

I believe it desirable, not so much with reference to the
local needs of the District, but to the great and lasting benefit
of the entire country, that this system [the public school system of the District of Columbia] should be crowned with a

[17] U. S., Congress, *Congressional Record*, 43 Cong., 1 sess., vol. 2, pt. 1:17–18.

university in all respects in keeping with the National Capital, and thereby realize the cherished hopes of Washington on this subject.[18]

Interest in a national university seems to have followed the cycles of more general interest in federal support of education. The period of the 1880's and 1890's offers a good case in point. Increased pressure for federal support of common schools and land-grant colleges, as well as a revival of interest in a national university, occurred during these years. The principal agent of the renewed interest in a national university was John W. Hoyt, a one-time governor of Wyoming and president of the University of Wyoming.

Hoyt authored the Senate bill, introduced on May 14, 1890, by Senator George Edmunds of Vermont, which contained many of the elements of the Sawyer bill of 1872.[19] The bill provided that the proposed university would carry on a program of education and research in many subjects but especially in those areas not already serviced by existing institutions. Control would rest in a board of ten high government officials, including the president and the secretary of the treasury, and twelve citizens appointed by Congress. Proposed public finance included a federal grant of $500,000.

Most significantly, the Senate did not refer the bill to the regular Committee on Education and Labor, but instead to a committee especially created to receive all proposals dealing with a national university. The committee, entitled "The Committee to Establish the University of the United States," approved the basic plan of the Edmunds bill and reported back the bill, or ones similar to it, with recommendations in 1890, 1893, 1894, 1896, 1899, and 1902.

Since 1894, Congress has received twenty-six bills in the Senate and seventeen in the House in support of a national university, but none has successfully passed both houses.[20] The great growth of the nation's colleges and universities has

18 Ibid., 45 Cong., 2 sess., vol. 7, pt. 1:7.
19 Ibid., 51 Cong., 1 sess., vol. 21, pt. 5:4643.
20 Madsen, *The National University*, pp. 167–69.

hindered the founding of a competing national institution, and the idea of a national university has been vigorously and successfully opposed by such leading educators as Presidents Charles W. Eliot of Harvard and Nicholas M. Butler of Columbia. Moreover, the increasing commitment to research which the proponents of the national university have urged as the principal function of the institution ran counter to the idea of broadening educational opportunity which came increasingly to characterize federal aid to education.

The debate on the constitutional aspects of federal aid to education has continued into the present and has involved higher as well as secondary and elementary education. Opponents of federal aid have traditionally charged the federal government as an interloper, aggressively usurping the prerogatives of the states and violating the constitutional doctrines of the government of delegated powers expressed in the reservations of the Tenth Amendment. Those supporting federal aid have taken the position that federal authority in educational matters was not mentioned through inadvertence but is implied in the Constitution in the "necessary and proper" and "general welfare" clauses. They argue that federal power remained latent and inoperative not because its existence was unrecognized but because the occasion and the popular demand for its use had not yet arisen. Thus the report of the National Advisory Committee on Education, established by President Hoover in 1931, found fourteen possible constitutional warrants for federal support of education.[21]

Constitutional objections of politically powerful congressmen made it necessary for those proposing educational legislation to exercise restraint even though, from the point of view of public policy, the legislation may have been desirable. Therefore, in drafting educational legislation it sometimes has been necessary to describe programs in such a way as to reduce constitutional objections and to combine aid to education with

[21] David S. Hill and William A. Fisher, *Basic Facts*, pt. 2 of *Federal Relations to Education—Report of the National Advisory Committee on Education* (Washington, D. C., 1931), 4–9.

collateral objectives. The 1958 National Defense Education Act illustrates this stratagem.

Such collateral objectives seem to have been present in much of the historic concern of national figures for the establishment of a national university. For example, Washington urged founding such an institution because he believed it would serve several substantial national needs. First, he deplored sending American youth abroad for university education because he deprecated "the hazard attending ardent and susceptible minds, from being too strongly and too early prepossessed in favor of other political systems, before they are capable of appreciating their own."[22] Second, he sought to reduce local prejudices and sectionalism: "Amongst the motives to such an institution the assimilation of principles, opinions, and manners of our countrymen, by the common education of a portion of our youth from every quarter, well deserves attention. The most homogeneous our citizens can be made in these particulars, the greater will be our prospect of permanent union. . . ." Third, he urged the promotion of political education as a national safeguard: "a primary object of such a national institution should be the education of our youth in the science of Government. In a Republic, what species of knowledge can be equally important, and what duty more pressing on its Legislature, than to patronize a plan for communicating it to those who are to be the future guardians of the liberties of the country?"[23]

Jefferson, like Washington, saw education functioning to bind together the various sections of the country in the same manner as would internal improvements. In his sixth message to Congress, December 2, 1806, he urged that the excess revenues of the federal government be applied to public improvement, including education, roads, rivers, and canals: "By these operations new channels of communication will be opened between the States; the lines of separation will disap-

---

[22] "Washington's Words on a National University," *Old South Leaflets*, 4, no. 76 (Boston, n.d.), 5.

[23] *Annals of Congress*, 4 Cong., 2 sess., 1595.

pear; their interests will be identified and their Union cemented by new and indissoluble ties."[24]

Discussing the accumulated surplus in the Treasury, Jefferson asked in his last annual message: "Shall it lie unproductive in the public vaults? Shall the revenue be reduced? Or, shall it not rather be appropriated to the improvement of roads, canals, rivers, education, and other great foundations of prosperity and union, under the powers which Congress may already possess, or such amendment of the Constitution as may be approved by the States?"[25]

Jefferson recognized the validity of the reasons for the Tenth Amendment's reservation of all nondelegated powers to the states. He urged, however, that the excess revenues of the federal government be applied to education, among other purposes:

> Education is here placed among the articles of public care, not that it would be proposed to take the ordinary branches out of the hands of private enterprise, which manages so much better all the concerns to which it is equal; but a public institution can alone supply those sciences which, though rarely called for, are yet necessary to complete the circle, all the parts of which contribute to the improvement of the country, and some of them to its preservation.[26]

In spite of the prestige and persuasiveness of its supporters, a national university failed to materialize. On the plot of ground which Washington set aside for its use now stands the National Observatory. Strict construction views of the constitutional power of the federal government prevented the creation of a national system of education. The nation was to have many state-oriented educational systems instead of a single national one. Instead of directly supporting national educational institutions, federal aid had to be channeled through the state governments or directed to the support of state colleges and universities. As the public lands provided the chief resource

[24] Ibid., 9 Cong., 2 sess., 14.
[25] Ibid., 10 Cong., 2 sess., 15.
[26] Ibid., 9 Cong., 2 sess., 14–15.

of the United States in the nineteenth century, the government first achieved support of these state institutions with grants of public lands. Securing the educational reservations in the western land grants of the federal government represented a major educational enterprise of the Founding Fathers.

3. PUBLIC LANDS AND SUPPORT OF EDUCATION

.

The idea of a national system of education was rejected early in our federal history. Education continued as a local concern, with the exception of certain specialized programs uniquely devoted to federal activities. But the question of the relationship of the federal government to education in the states continued. Should the federal government assist education in the states, and if so, what resources could the federal government use and how would they be distributed? Were all the states to benefit or only some? The cumulative effect of certain events beginning in the revolutionary period led to the development of a program which answered some of these questions by tying federal support of education to the federal land policy.

The Mississippi River became the boundary between the British and Spanish possessions in North America by virtue of the Treaty of Paris in 1763. When the colonies declared their independence, the same river marked the claimed western limit of their territory. None of the western land was in the public domain of the federal government, however, for individual states claimed the entire area under various and conflicting titles.

Among the states without claims, Maryland first took action to force cession of the western land to the central government by refusing to ratify the Articles of Confederation until such cession was guaranteed. In consequence, on October 10, 1780, Congress pledged that all land ceded "shall be disposed of for the common benefit of the United States."[1] All states made

---

[1] *Journals of the American Congress, 1774–1788* (Washington, D. C., 1823), 3:535.

commitments to cede their western lands, although Virginia retained all the territory that eventually became the state of Kentucky, and North Carolina reserved claims to a large part of the territory that became the state of Tennessee. However, satisfied with the commitments made, Maryland ratified the Articles on March 1, 1781. Actual conveyance of title by the states to the United States took place from 1781 to 1802, with New York and Virginia leading the way in 1781 and 1783, respectively.

While Congress was considering the conditions of the Virginia cession proposal, a group of New Englanders headed by Colonel Timothy Pickering and General Rufus Putnam conceived of forming a new state in the Northwest Territory to be settled by New England veterans and their families under their revolutionary war bounty rights. Pickering wrote to a Colonel Hodgbon on April 7, 1783, referring to the plan of government for the proposed state. The significant features included an agreement on a constitution and form of government, the total and constitutional exclusion of slavery, and the admission of the state as an equal member of the Confederation. The following significant language from the proposal concerned education: "All surplus lands shall be the common property of the State and disposed of for the common good; as for laying our roads, building bridges, erecting public buildings, establishing schools and academies, defraying the expenses of government, and other public uses."[2]

General Washington forwarded the proposal (known as the Army Plan) to Congress on June 17, 1783, and urged that it be enacted into law. In Washington's mind, a settlement of army men would make an ideal frontier community.[3] Congress failed to act, but the proposal had significance in that it represented the first official plan proposing a national dedication of public lands for the support of education.

[2] Octavius Pickering, *The Life of Timothy Pickering* (Boston, 1867–1873), 1:457.

[3] George Bancroft, *History of the Formation of the Constitution of the United States of America* (New York, 1884), 1:315–16.

Public Lands and Education

In an effort to bring consideration of the conditions of the Virginia cession proposal to a head, Theodorick Bland, a Virginia delegate to Congress, twelve days earlier had submitted an alternative plan for the settlement of the Northwest. In a motion, seconded by Alexander Hamilton of New York, Bland moved that Congress accept the Virginia cession proposal under which the ceded land would be divided into districts in which Continental soldiers would receive bounty lands. His motion, on June 5, 1783, continued:

> And be it further ordained, that out of every hundred thousand acres so granted there shall be reserved as a domain for the use of the United States ten thousand acres, each of which ten thousand acres shall remain forever a common property of the United States, unalienable but by the consent of the United States in congress assembled; the rents, shares, profits, and produce of which lands, when any such shall arise, to be appropriated to the payment of the civil list of the United States, the erecting of frontier forts, the founding of seminaries of learning, and the surplus after such purposes (if any) to be appropriated to the building and equipping of a navy, and to no other use or purpose whatever.[4]

Bland's motion failed to carry, and after some debate the proposal, known as the Financiers' Plan, died in committee.

A comparison of the Army and the Financiers' plans reveals interesting differences which characterized proposed educational uses of the public lands. The Army Plan would have fixed on new states the institutions of New England. These included an agreement on the form of government as a condition precedent to settlement, an antislavery constitution, and the township-platting system of local government. The Financiers' Plan made no mention of such controversial items. Settlement of the area under consideration represented the prime objective primarily because it would produce the cash needed to help pay the public debt. Attaching conditions to settlement appeared to be a luxury the nation could not afford.

4 Ibid., 313–14.

As a secondary matter both plans included provisions for the use of public lands for support of education. Both designated education as one of the ordinary and necessary expenses of government. Drawn by the citizens who proposed to settle in the territory under consideration, the Army Plan provided that education should come under the control of the state, with the land dedicated to education being reserved to the state. The drafters of the Financiers' Plan reserved the land to the central government to insure that education would come under national control.

Alexander Hamilton accurately characterized the different objectives in the plans when in his July 20, 1790, report to Congress on a "Plan for the Disposition of the Public Lands" he noted

> that in the formation of a plan for the disposition of the vacant lands of the United States there appear to be two leading objects of consideration; one, the facility of advantageous sales, according to the probable course of purchases; the other the accommodation of individuals now inhabiting the western country, or who may emigrate thither hereafter. The former, as an operation of finance, claims primary attention . . . .[5]

After the treaty of 1783 ended the war, the westward movement increased, and Congress received great pressure to provide some political organization for the western territory. On March 1, 1784, a committee headed by Thomas Jefferson reported an ordinance for the temporary organization and government of the new territory. The primary issues faced by the committee had to do with the extent of congressional control over and responsibility for the western territory, the definition of the method by which new states could be created out of the territory, and the relationship of these new states to the existing states.[6] Adopted as an ordinance on April 23, 1784, it

[5] Quoted in *House Executive Document 47*, 46 Cong., 3 sess., pt. 4: 198 [Report of the Public Lands Commissioner, 1880].
[6] Merrill D. Peterson, *Thomas Jefferson and the New Nation* (New York, 1970), 281.

32

made no provision for the sale of land to settlers, nor did it make any provision for reservation of land for education, but it had great importance in nationalizing the Northwest.[7]

Jefferson then submitted, on May 28, 1784, "an ordinance for ascertaining the mode of locating and disposing of lands in the western territory."[8] The measure included complete directions for the survey of land and the method and terms of its sale, although again without mention of any reservation for education. This omission is surprising in light of the great concern for education so properly attributed to Jefferson, and in light of the fact that the Army and Financiers' plans, which had been submitted to Congress several months previously, both included provisions for the support of education.[9]

Congress took no action on Jefferson's proposed land ordinance until the following year, at which time it referred the matter to a new committee with a member from each state. Jefferson, in the meantime, had withdrawn from Congress and on March 10, 1785, had been appointed minister to France.[10]

New Englanders raised many objections to Jefferson's plan. Timothy Pickering complained particularly of finding "no provision for ministers of the gospel, nor even for schools or academies, the latter at least might have been brought into view."[11] The ordinance as finally adopted on May 20, 1785, incorporated many of the provisions of Jefferson's bill but also added a significant new clause, as follows: "There shall be reserved the lot No. 16, of every township, for the maintenance of public schools, within the said township . . . ."[12] This first

[7] "Report of Government for the Western Territory," *Old South Leaflets*, 6, no. 127 (Boston, n.d.), 22–26.

[8] *Journals of the American Congress* 4:416.

[9] A reading of some of the principal biographies of Jefferson reveals no clear answer to this problem. A possible explanation is that the problems confronted by Jefferson in 1785 remained those that confronted him in 1784. Jefferson appeared primarily concerned with conceptualizing ideally the relationship and responsibilities of Congress to the new territory. (See n. 6, above.)

[10] *Journals of the American Congress* 4:478.

[11] Pickering to Rufus King, Mar. 8, 1785, *Life of Pickering* 1:509.

[12] *Journals of the American Congress* 4:521.

effective step in the direction of material assistance to education thus reflected the strong influence of New Englanders as well as that of Thomas Jefferson.[13]

Called the Land Ordinance of 1785, this legislation provided the stability and organization necessary to promote settlement in the Northwest; and soon after its passage, General Putnam decided to revive his scheme for settling New England soldiers there. Thus on January 10, 1786, he issued a circular proposing the formation of a company to promote this purpose. A group of interested men met in Boston on March 1, 1786, and signed thirteen articles of agreement, creating the body known as the Ohio Company of Associates. These articles reflected the influence of the Army Plan in the organization of government and in the exclusion of slavery. Participants of the Boston meeting elected stockholders and appointed a committee consisting of Manasseh Cutler, General William Parsons, and General Rufus Putnam to apply to Congress for the private purchase of lands.

The Land Ordinance of 1785 established the official practice with regard to the size or parcels and credit provisions for the sale of public lands in the Northwest. This practice included public auction at a minimum price of one dollar an acre, plus the costs of survey and other charges rated at thirty-six dollars a township. Mr. Cutler thought the price set by the ordinance too high and suggested that Congress provide for survey at government expense and then charge the company not more than fifty cents an acre.[14]

Cutler was clearly in a position to bring a certain amount of pressure to bear on Congress. Because of the unsettled nature of the times, western land sales had been slow, and Congress faced an ever-growing need for revenue. This need could best be satisfied by the sale of substantial portions of the west-

[13] All the actions of the Confederation Congress were subsequently given the force of law as against the federal government by act of the new Congress and provision of the Constitution.

[14] William Parker Cutler and Julia Perkins Cutler, *Life, Journals, and Correspondence of Reverend Manasseh Cutler* (Cincinnati, 1888), 1:193.

ern domain, and the Ohio Company proposed sale of 1 million acres, although at a price lower than what Congress thought desirable.

The government of the Northwest, as established by the Ordinance of 1784, was temporary by definition. Moreover, Monroe, appointed by Congress in 1786 chairman of a new committee to revise the ordinance, questioned many of Jefferson's assumptions as to size, number, and nature of the subdivisions proposed under the ordinance.

The work of Monroe's committee, later chaired by William Johnson of Connecticut, together with the pressure of the Ohio Company, resulted in the passage of the Northwest Ordinance of July 17, 1787.[15] This famous ordinance provided a plan for government for the area later carved into the states of Ohio, Indiana, Illinois, Michigan, Wisconsin, and that part of Minnesota lying east of the Mississippi. Again, the New England influence was evident in the exclusion of slavery and the other articles of company dealing with the territorial form of government. The ordinance dealt not so much with land policy as with a system of government and therefore included no reservations of any kind in support of education or religion. It did, however, include the now familiar words of the Third Article of Compact: "Religion, morality, and knowledge, being necessary to good government and the happiness of mankind, schools and the means of education shall forever be encouraged."[16] Although these words have over the years had enormous effect as expressions of an ideology, they have never had any force of law.

Even though a favorable plan of government had been secured, the Ohio Company, the largest prospective buyer, still had the problem of purchasing the land. Cutler's first proposal called for a reservation of one section out of thirty-six in each township for support of the common schools, one township for the support of the ministry, and four townships for the

[15] Jack Ericson Eblen, *The First and Second United States Empires* (Pittsburgh, 1968), 28–51.

[16] *Statutes at Large* 1 (1787):51.

establishment of a university.[17] Congress countered with a proposed agreement reserving only Section 16 for schools, as provided in the ordinance of 1785. Cutler then reduced his demands to the minimum acceptable to him, including the reservation of Section 16 for the maintenance of schools, Section 29 for religion, and not more than two townships for a university. Before these terms could be accepted, Cutler had to agree to a secret proposal of the secretary of the board of the treasury, Colonel William Duer, to expand the size of the proposed contract of the Ohio Company to 5 million acres, which included land to be bought by the Scioto Company formed by Duer's friends.[18] As a result of this combination of compromises and threats by Cutler to break off negotiations with Congress and purchase Maine lands from his own state, the Congress finally agreed to the Ohio Company offer. On July 23, 1787, Congress authorized the board of the Treasury to complete contracts for the sale of nearly 5 million acres of land at a price that amounted to about nine cents an acre.[19]

The provisions of the sale marked a substantial advance over any legislative action discussed so far in that they included the following reservations of land for the support of higher education: "Not more than two complete townships to be given perpetually for the purposes of an university, to be laid off by the purchaser or purchasers, as near the centre as may be, so that the same shall be of good land, to be applied to the intended objects by the legislature of the state."[20]

On October 27, 1787, Cutler signed two contracts purchas-

[17] George W. Knight, "History and Management of Federal Land Grants for Education in the Northwest Territory," *Papers of the American Historical Association*, 1, no. 3 (1886), 88–89.

[18] Cutler and Cutler, *Life, Journals, and Correspondence* 1:293, 303.

[19] Payson Jackson Treat, *The National Land System, 1785–1820* (New York, 1910), 51. The quoted price was one dollar an acre. A discount of one-third was allowed for bad land and incidental charges. Payment could be made in certificates of indebtedness then worth only about twelve cents on the dollar. Military bounty rights, also acquired at substantial discount, could be offered up to one-seventh of the whole amount.

[20] *Journals of Congress*, 4, app., p. 17.

ing 1.5 million acres for the Ohio Company and securing an option for the Scioto Company to purchase from 3.5 million to 5 million acres.[21]

Inspired in part by the success of the Ohio Company, John Cleve Symmes in August of the same year petitioned Congress for a purchase of 1 million acres of land lying between the two Miami rivers. Symmes, however, asked for only one township for an academy instead of the two townships for a university requested by Cutler.[22] In August Congress authorized the sale to Symmes. But before Symmes could sign his contract, Congress decided not to reserve any more lands for academies or seminaries in private contracts unless the purchases were at least as large as that of the Ohio Company and in some prospective state other than Ohio.[23] Thus, Symmes's contract, signed subsequent to this congressional action, contained no reservation for an academy. Symmes executed his contract and acquired the land but without any reservations for higher education. Congress did not reverse its position until May 5, 1792, at which time it granted Symmes one township for an academy.[24]

It was not immediately certain from all these transactions whether Congress had established a policy of support of higher education or had merely made several isolated grants as a kind of bonus, for those most likely to purchase, to stimulate sales of land so this natural resource could be turned to cash. On the one hand, the language in the Northwest Ordinance about the desirability of supporting education, it must be emphasized, had no force in law.[25] The Southwest Ordinance of May 26, 1790, in very general language, extended the terms of the Northwest Ordinance, except the slavery exclusion to the area

---

[21] Howard Cromwell Taylor, *The Educational Significance of the Early Federal Land Ordinances* (New York, 1922), 29.

[22] *Journals of Congress*, 4, app., p. 18.

[23] Ibid., 802–803.

[24] *Annals of Congress*, 2 Cong., 2 sess., 1373–74.

[25] Professor W. H. Cowley of Stanford University has emphasized this point in numerous lectures and articles.

south of the Ohio.[26] But this extension merely provided a convenient way of providing for the temporary government of a newly ceded area and served much the same purpose as the Ordinance of 1784. Neither of these measures, dealing with the nature and form of proposed government and not with land policy, included any reservations or grants. On the other hand, the Land Ordinance of 1785 did reserve one section in each township for the support of schools.[27]

Yet the first actual grant of land for schools and for higher education originated not in a general ordinance but in the provisions for specific land sales in 1787. The first university grant represented simply one feature of a private bargain between Congress and the business representatives of a commercial company. The weight of evidence, therefore, seems to indicate that prior to 1800, Congress had little concern for support of education that was not tied to the question of the sale of public lands.

The seed of a policy had been planted, however, in the specific sales of the public lands discussed. Before the principles underlying these sales could be more widely applied, they came seriously into question in the circumstances surrounding the admission of Ohio, the first state created in the Northwest.

---

[26] 1 *Statutes at Large of the United States of America, 1789–*, 123 (1790).

[27] The township system with its educational reservations was defended because it made for the kind of compact settlement that encouraged sales of land, while the Southern method of indiscriminate surveys of small tracts was claimed to have a tendency to "destroy all those inducements to emigration which are derived from friendships, religion, and relative connections . . . ." Treat, *National Land System*, 31.

4. LAND GRANTS FOR EDUCATION

IN THE NEW STATES

.

Article VI, paragraph 1 of the Constitution of the United States guaranteed the validity of "all Debts contracted and Engagements entered into" by the Confederation Congress, thereby making the land reservations and grants of 1785 and 1787 binding upon the federal government. And with General Anthony Wayne's defeat of the Indians at the battle of Fallen Timbers in 1794, the Northwest was "pacified" for white settlers. Thus with the form of government established, the system of land disposal determined, and the frontier secured, the westward movement began in earnest.

By 1799 the townships reserved for higher education under the Ohio Contract had been located, surveyed, and settled, and after a five-year rent-free period were expected to produce rental income of over $5,000.[1] As the process of settlement continued, territories sought additional grants for education. From 1799 to 1802, settlers in the Southwest Territory petitioned Congress for grants similar to those secured in the Northwest. Settlers in the Northwest petitioned for additional grants for academies, colleges, and seminaries.[2] On January 2, 1802, the territorial legislature of Ohio chartered American Western University (which in 1804 became Ohio University), using the educational land grant in the 1787 contract as the principal source of income.

---

[1] Cutler and Cutler, *Life, Journals, and Correspondence*, 2:18–19.
[2] *Annals of Congress*, 6 Cong., 1 sess., 153; 7 Cong., 1 sess., 497, 949.

In 1802, when the territorial legislature of Ohio applied to Congress for admission to the Union as a new state, it proposed that title to all the reserved land in the territory which was then vested in the United States should be vested in the new state. The discussion of the Ohio proposal in Congress focused attention on the entire matter of federal support of education. The question at issue was whether the reservations secured by contract in 1787 should form the basis of a general federal policy of supporting education by means of land grants, or whether these grants should be considered as merely isolated legislative enactments involved only with specific sales of land.

Those who opposed the Ohio proposal also rejected the idea of a broad federal policy of support. Their arguments recited the following points. First, a federal statute, passed in 1790, had guaranteed the proceeds from the sale of western lands as a sinking fund for use in discharging the public debt of the United States.[3] Therefore, no additional land should be granted for support of education until the debt had been extinguished. Second, the express wording of the Virginia cession required that the ceded land be used for the benefit of all the states. Third, Indian titles to lands in the Northwest had been extinguished by funds from the federal treasury to which all the states had contributed. Therefore, no new state should be allowed to benefit, to the exclusion of the others, by virtue of a grant of lands acquired for the common benefit with common funds.

As principal spokesman for this position, Congressman Andrew Gregg of Pennsylvania asked:

> With what face of justice can we then put our hands into this common fund, or lay hold of any portion of these lands, and apply them to the use and benefit of the people of one part of the country, to the entire exclusion of the rest, as is contemplated by this bill? . . . It appeared to him an as-

[3] 1 *Stat.* 144 (1790).

sumption of power which did not of right belong to them. It was an act of usurpation which he had not been able to discover any principle whatsoever to warrant or justify.[4]

Congressman John Randolph of Virginia spoke for those who advocated accepting the Ohio proposal. His argument did not rest on the desirability of education but rather on the grounds that donations of land for educational purposes would increase the value of the adjacent properties and hence attract more settlers. "Can we suppose that emigration will not be promoted by it, and that the value of lands will not be enhanced by the emigrant obtaining the fullest education for his children; and is it not better to receive two dollars an acre with an appropriation for schools, than seventy-five cents an acre without such appropriation?"[5]

After much debate, Congress agreed to grant to Ohio Section 16 of every township for support of common schools, certain salt springs and the adjacent saline lands, and one-twentieth of the net proceeds of the sales of public lands for the building of roads and other internal improvements. In return, the territorial legislature had to agree to a five-year tax exemption for lands sold by the federal government within the state so that no third party could acquire a tax default title before the United States had secured the full purchase price under the then prevailing five-year credit sales system. The Ohio territorial legislature accepted these terms on condition that Congress extend the school and university reservations to cover the military districts and reserves within the state. All terms were agreed to, and Congress passed the Ohio Enabling Act on April 30, 1802.[6] On March 3, 1803, Congress passed a supplementary act vesting in the state school lands reserved in the Virginia Reservation and the Connecticut Reserve. The act also vested the one township for the support of an academy

[4] *Annals of Congress*, 7 Cong., 2 sess., 585.
[5] Ibid., 586–87.
[6] 2 *Stat.* 173 (1802).

(college) secured by the Symmes contract, which became the basic endowment for Miami University.[7]

Subsequent observers might say with President Franklin Pierce that these grants to Ohio could be looked upon as the "acts of a mere land-owner disposing of a small share of his property in a way to augment the value of the residue, and in this mode to encourage the early occupation of it by the industrious and intelligent pioneer."[8] However, this appraisal would not account for the school lands granted in the Connecticut and Virginia reserves, where the federal government sold no land. Moreover, even if Congress acted merely as a prudent landowner, the congressional committee reporting favorably on the 1802 Ohio admission bill felt it necessary to justify its finding because of the desirability "of acceding to a proposition, the tendency of which is to cherish and confirm our present happy political institutions and habits."[9] Still it was necessary to couch the grants in a form of a contract in order to achieve congressional approval, and the tax concession became an important element of the subsequent grant policy. Thus the admission of Ohio established the several precedents for a policy under which the federal government has contracted to assist every public-land state with land grants for support of secondary and higher education.

This policy was first of all a compromise. The grants represented bargains with the new states more than outright gifts. Education was considered in much the same manner as internal improvements. In the policy associated with the admission of new states, the federal government made grants not only for education but also for road construction and other internal improvements. The public debt could be more rapidly paid off if settlers could be induced to purchase land. The gifts

---

[7] Ibid., 225 (1803).

[8] U. S., Congress, Senate, *Journal of the Senate of the United States*, 33 Cong., 1 sess., 368.

[9] *American State Papers. Documents Legislative and Executive, of the Congress of the United States* (Washington, D. C., 1834), misc. vol. 1:340–41.

of salt springs, saline lands, and the 5 percent fund for internal improvements became a part of the bonus received by the settlers, along with the educational grants.

The absence of federal supervision of the management of land granted and the absence of any restrictions regarding its use became another precedent established by the admission of Ohio. Once the national government made a land grant, it refrained from exercising any control over management of the land. Fee title was vested in the states so that education, even though federally endowed, was not federally controlled. Congress introduced exceptions to this general rule after the Civil War, but then only because inefficient management, and in some cases outright fraud, prevented the federal grants from achieving anything but minimal usefulness.

The federal government made no effort to designate the subject matter taught or the nature of the institution receiving the land endowment other than that the grants generally went to "the state university." The support of the state university (or in some subsequent cases "seminary") in the Ohio bill represented still another precedent. The language of the 1787 contract provided that the land grants were "to be applied to the intended object by the legislature of the state." Thus when American Western University (Ohio University) received its charter in 1802, the territorial legislature turned over to the university board of trustees the two townships granted to the Ohio Company. The legislature retained only the power to "alter, limit, or restrain any of the powers granted" to the institution, and it required the university to make annual reports. Ohio University, the oldest institution for higher education in the Old Northwest, and the first to be endowed with funds derived from national land grants for education, became also the first state university in the Old Northwest.

It has been shown above that the movement for the establishment of state universities in the new states received initial impetus and important financial backing from the federal government. A statement confirming this fact in the charter of the University of Alabama reads, "the University of Alabama was called into existence by the generosity of Congress."[10]

The precedents established by Congress in the admission of Ohio soon became the settled policy of the federal government. Congress reserved school, seminary, university, and college lands during the territorial period or in the Enabling Act, and then vested them in the state upon its admission to the Union or soon thereafter. With the exception of five states, every state entering the Union after the forming of the Constitution benefited from such educational grants or their equivalent. Four states not in the public domain—Maine, Kentucky, Vermont, and West Virginia—were carved out of states which had been among the original thirteen colonies. The fifth, Texas, retained title to all the public land within its boundaries on its admission to the Union and therefore contained no public land for the United States to grant.

As a general rule, Congress conveyed to each of the public-land states two townships (seventy-two sections, or 46,080 acres) for the support of higher education in addition to the other grants first detailed in the Ohio Enabling Act. The case of Michigan will serve as an example. In 1804, Congress created three new districts out of the remainder of the Northwest Territory and in each of these districts reserved a township for the support of higher education.[11] These districts ultimately became the territories of Indiana, Illinois, and Michigan, each of which received a grant of an additional township during its territorial era.

Then on May 20, 1826, Congress passed an act reserving certain land in the territory of Michigan for the use of a university as follows:

> that the Secretary of the Treasury be, and he is hereby, authorized to set apart and reserve from sale, out of any of the public lands within the territory of Michigan, to which

[10] Donald G. Tewksbury, *The Founding of American Colleges and Universities Before the Civil War* (New York, 1932), 184.
[11] 2 *Stat.* 277 (1804).

44

Indian title may be extinguished, and not otherwise appropriated, a quantity of land, not exceeding two entire townships, for the use and support of an university within the territory aforesaid, and for no other use or purpose whatever, to be located in tracts of land corresponding with any of the legal divisions into which the public lands are authorized to be surveyed, not less than one section one of which said townships, so set apart and reserved from sale, shall be in lieu of an entire township of land, directed to be located in said territory for the use of a seminary of learning therein, by an act of Congress entitled "An Act making provision for the disposal of the public lands in the Indiana territory, and for other purposes," approved March twenty-sixth, one-thousand eight-hundred and four.[12]

The act of June 23, 1836, providing for the admission of Michigan to the Union, vested the reserved lands in the state.

That the seventy-two sections of land set apart and reserved for the use and support of a university by an act of Congress approved on the twentieth day of May, eighteen hundred and twenty-six, entitled "An Act concerning a seminary of learning in the Territory of Michigan," are hereby granted and conveyed to the State, to be appropriated solely to the use and support of such university, in such manner as the Legislature may prescribe. . . .[13]

Several of the states admitted before 1850 were exceptions to the general rule of a reservation and grant of two townships. Tennessee entered the Union in 1796 without benefit of educational grants. On April 18, 1806, Congress ceded to Tennessee all outstanding claims of the federal government to lands within the eastern portion of the state. In exchange, Tennessee conceded to a five-year tax exemption for public lands in the remainder of the state and agreed to perfect all of the North Carolina warrants within the state and to set aside 100,000 acres for the support of two colleges.[14]

---

[12] 4 *Stat.* 180 (1826).
[13] 5 *Stat.* 59 (1836).
[14] 2 *Stat.* 381 (1806).

Louisiana received as the Orleans Territory reservations of two townships for support of higher education in 1806 and 1811. Congress confirmed these grants not in the Enabling Act in 1812 but in a subsequent act in 1827.[15] Indiana received an additional township at the time of admission in 1816. This reservation became the subject of litigation, with the United States Supreme Court deciding against the state in 1853 in the case of *Trustees for Vincennes University* v. *the State of Indiana* (12 Howard 268). To compensate for the failure of title to this township, Congress granted 19,040 acres to the state in 1854 for the exclusive use of the state university.[16]

Florida, admitted in 1845, and Wisconsin, admitted in 1846, received special treatment. Florida acquired additional townships for two seminaries in an act supplementary to its act of admission.[17] Wisconsin, carved out of the territory of Illinois, had not received a township reservation in the 1804 grant to the districts of the Indiana territory since no fourth state had been contemplated at that time. Congress, therefore, made a grant of two townships in 1838 during the territorial era and confirmed them in the Enabling Act of 1846. In 1854, Wisconsin received seventy-two additional sections for support of the university.[18]

In addition to the general land grants associated with the admission of states, Congress also established a series of special-purpose grants of certain kinds of lands or proceeds from the sale of lands. The earliest of these grants, the Saline Grants, dated from the admission of Ohio.

Under the Land Law of 1796, the United States reserved title to all salt springs in the public domain, along with the six adjacent sections. Beginning with Ohio, each Enabling Act offered this saline land to the new state on condition that it be selected within a year of admission. Most states fulfilled

[15] 4 *Stat.* 244 (1827).
[16] 10 *Stat.* 267 (1854).
[17] 5 *Stat.* 788 (1845).
[18] 10 *Stat.* 597 (1854).

this requirement, and Congress conveyed more than 600,000 acres under this program, a part of which went to support education.[19]

The Five Per Cent Grants, made first in 1803, and the Internal Improvement Grants dating from 1841, were given to the new states for various internal improvements. The former was based on a percentage of the value of the public lands within the state, and the latter on a grant of 500,000 acres to each new state. The states received more than $19 million and 7 million acres from these two sources, and again a part of this grant went to support education.[20]

However, by far the largest of the special grants were the Swamp and Overflow grants begun in 1850, under which the states have received almost 65 million acres from the federal government.[21] By the terms of these acts, the federal government conveyed to the state for reclamation land designated on the plats of the government surveys as swamp or river-flood areas and therefore unfit for cultivation. Again, much of the proceeds from the subsequent sale of this reclaimed land went for support of education and other public purposes.

Beginning in 1889 with the Enabling Act for North and South Dakota, Montana, and Washington, the pattern as established by the Ohio Enabling Act and the specific acts mentioned above underwent radical change. To each of these states admitted from 1889 to 1911, Congress granted the Five Per Cent fund specifically for "support of the common schools" in recognition of the fact that many states receiving the grant in the past had applied a large portion of it to education. Then, under Section 17 of the 1889 act, Congress replaced the Saline, the Swamp Land and Overflow, and the Internal Improvement grants with a single grant of 500,000 acres for each of the states admitted under the act, designated for

[19] U. S., General Land Office, *School Lands—Land Grants to States and Territories for Educational Purposes* (Washington, D. C., 1939), 3–11.

[20] U. S., Bureau of Land Management, *Public Land Statistics, 1963* (Washington, D. C., 1963), 6–7.

[21] Ibid., *1965*, 8.

specific institutions.[22] Congress here began to exercise for the first time some control over the use of the land granted.

South Dakota and Montana had previously received grants of two townships for their universities.[23] Under the terms of Section 17 of the 1889 act, South Dakota received 40,000 more acres for the state university, 40,000 acres for a school of mines, 80,000 acres for normal schools, and 340,000 acres for other institutional, general educational, and charitable purposes. North Dakota received the same quantity of land for similar purposes, although all 86,080 acres for the university were granted in 1889. For support of higher education, Montana in 1889 received 100,000 acres for a school of mines and 100,000 acres for normal schools. The other 300,000 acres were for other institutional purposes. Washington obtained 500,000 acres, including 46,080 for the state university, 100,000 acres for "establishment and maintenance of a scientific school," 100,000 acres for normal schools, and 200,000 acres for general education and charitable purposes. Section 17 of the act then concluded as follows:

> That the States provided for in this act shall not be entitled to any further or other grants of land for any purpose than as expressly provided in this act. And the lands granted by this section shall be held, appropriated, and disposed of exclusively for the purpose herein mentioned, in such manner as the legislatures of the respective States may severally provide.

Colorado, admitted in 1876, was the first state whose Enabling Act provided a minimum sale price for the public lands granted at the time of admission. Section 11 of the 1889 act discussed above raised that minimum sale price from $2.50 an acre to $10.00 an acre.

Section 14 of the 1889 act introduced a clause which for the first time required that federal grants be used to support only state institutions. The language was as follows:

[22] 25 *Stat.* 676 (1889).
[23] 21 *Stat.* 326 (1881).

> The schools, colleges, and universities provided for in this
> act shall forever remain under the exclusive control of the
> said States, respectively, and no part of the proceeds arising
> from the sale or disposal of any lands herein granted for
> educational purposes shall be used for the support of any
> sectarian or denominational school, college, or university.

The grant of the Five Per Cent fund for education, the denominational clause, the clause establishing a minimum sale
price and certain leasing stipulations, and the grants for specific institutions—in lieu of the general grants for internal
improvements, swamp lands, salt springs, and saline lands—
continued to be elements of the federal educational grants
program for new states.

Wyoming, admitted in 1890, had also received 46,080
acres for a university in 1881; and there were no specific
grants for higher education in the total acreage granted at
admission. Idaho, on the other hand, already had a university
at Moscow; and Congress, at the time of admission in 1890,
designated 50,000 acres for support of that institution in addition to the two townships granted during the territorial stage.
Idaho also obtained 100,000 acres for normal schools and
100,000 acres for scientific schools.[24]

The Enabling Act for Utah, passed in 1894, contained the
most liberal grants that Congress had made up to that time
because of the lower average value of mountain and desert
land. Utah received 100,000 acres for the university, in addition to the 46,080 acres received during the territorial period
in 1855.[25] The state also received an additional grant of
100,000 acres—including the saline lands—for support of
the university, and 100,000 acres for normal schools, for a
total of 650,000 acres instead of the normal 500,000 acres.
This acreage included a grant of 100,000 acres for a school
of mines to be connected with the university.[26]

[24] 26 *Stat.* 215, 222 (1890).
[25] 10 *Stat.* 611 (1855).
[26] 28 *Stat.* 107 (1894).

Congress continued the policy of more generous donations of land in the cases of the dry-land states of Oklahoma, Arizona, and New Mexico. The 1906 Enabling Act for Oklahoma granted over 1,050,000 acres, including 250,000 acres for the University of Oklahoma, 300,000 acres for normal schools, and 100,000 acres for "The Colored Agricultural and Normal University." Education also received support from a special fund created out of the sale of every Section 13 open for settlement, with one-third going to the normal schools, one-third to the agricultural and mechanical college, and one-third to "The Colored Agricultural and Normal University."[27]

Arizona received 46,080 acres for a university in 1881, along with Montana, Idaho, South Dakota, and Wyoming. New Mexico had been generously treated in 1898 in receiving 111,080 acres for a university, 100,000 acres for normal schools, 50,000 acres for a school of mines, and 50,000 acres for a military institute.[28] Arizona and New Mexico then received similar treatment in their 1910 Enabling Act. Each obtained 1,050,000 acres—including 200,000 acres for a university, 150,000 acres for a school of mines, and 100,000 acres for a military institute—and a separate fund of 1 million acres to be used to liquidate special bond issues passed at the request of the United States during their territorial period. Congress introduced a special requirement in the case of these two states in that each of the grants mentioned was to constitute a separate fund for bookkeeping purposes which could be invested only in "safe" securities.[29]

Alaska and Hawaii, the last two states to be admitted, presented special situations in that Alaska had enormous quantities of public land, and Hawaii had practically none. In 1915, during Alaska's territorial period, certain designated sections had been reserved for a territorial agricultural school and school of mines when established. Mineral rights and the proceeds of the sale of certain lands were also dedicated for general

27 34 *Stat.* 267 (1906).
28 30 *Stat.* 484 (1898).
29 36 *Stat.* 557 (1910).

support, and certain sections were reserved as a site for the institution.[30] In 1929, Congress added 100,000 acres to the fund established in 1915.[31] The 1958 act admitting Alaska provided further general support from the public lands for community and recreation activities. The Five Per Cent Grant for support of the public schools was continued, but there were no specific reservations of sections or townships for schools or colleges or for the Morrill Act provisions. Instead, Congress conveyed title to 102,550,000 acres of the public domain to the state for general educational and other related purposes. It was clear from the language of the act that Congress intended to support schools and colleges since the act included the denominational clause.[32]

Hawaii, admitted in 1959, received no specific grants during its territorial period. The act of July 7, 1898, establishing its territorial status, provided that Congress would enact special laws for the management and disposal of public lands. To this end, Congress subsequently assigned all revenue from these lands, including proceeds from their sale, for "educational and other public purposes."[33]

In the act providing for the admission of Hawaii, the United States granted

the United States title to all the public lands and other public property within the boundaries of the State of Hawaii, title to which is held by the United States immediately prior to its admission into the Union. The grant hereby made shall be in lieu of any and all grants provided for new States by provisions of law other than this Act, and such grants shall not extend to the State of Hawaii. . . . [These lands together with the proceeds from the sale thereof and the income therefrom] shall be held by said State as a public trust for the support of public schools and other public educational institutions . . . .[34]

[30] 38 *Stat.* 1214 (1915).
[31] 45 *Stat.* 1091 (1929).
[32] 72 *Stat.* 339 (1958).
[33] 30 *Stat.* 750 (1898).
[34] 73 *Stat.* 4 (1959).

In addition, Hawaii obtained a cash grant of $6 million under the 1960 Hawaii Omnibus Act in lieu of a Morrill Act land grant.

To complete this part of the story of federal land grants, mention must be made of three acts. In 1908, Congress passed the Forest Reserve Act under which states which contained forest reserves received 25 percent of the revenues derived from the leasing of these lands to private companies. The size of the income derived can be measured by the fact that in 1956 distributions totaled $27,939,000, of which it is estimated more than 50 percent went for support of education.[35]

The Mineral Leasing Act of 1920 provided the same kind of compensation to states in which the government leased mineral resources to private enterprise. While designed for conservation purposes, the funds so derived were in fact largely used for school support. California, for example, applied the receipts to a creation of a junior college fund.

The last major federal land-grant program was the Federal School Land Act of 1927, under which the states received title to all minerals on school lands. Under the terms of this and the earlier Mineral Leasing Act, more than $477 million has been made available to the states, a large part of which has gone to support education, particularly at the elementary school level.[36]

The statement has been made that "the basis on which the several federal land grants were given to the states fails to follow any logical pattern." Grants were made to the states equally or according to the size of the states, the population, the geological and geographic formation, and the value of the public lands. "The question of need was, for all purposes, ignored."[37]

[35] Marion Clawson and Burnett Held, *Federal Lands: Their Use and Management* (Baltimore, 1957), 413.

[36] *Public Land Statistics, 1963*, 185.

[37] George Donald Merrill, "Land and Education—The Origin and History of Land Grants for the Support of Education" (Ed.D. diss., University of Southern California, 1965), 22.

However true this statement may be, there is no doubt that these land grants provided the basis for the now substantial program of federal aid to both higher and secondary education. The importance of higher-education grants discussed in this chapter is often overlooked in comparison with the relatively better-known policy established under the Morrill Act of 1862. The grants were not made to all states but only to those carved out of the public domain.

As a consequence of all these limitations, pressure developed early in the nineteenth century in Congress to support education with grants of income from the proceeds of the sale of public lands or from general treasury funds rather than just with grants of land. Thus was the way opened for the present widespread program of federal assistance from a variety of funds to all states.

Finally, few states managed the endowments created by these grants in such a way as to return a significant income from them. In almost all cases, state universities originally supported by this landed endowment are presently receiving only limited funds from this source compared with the over-all size of their current budgets. An example of the consequence of the tying of support of education to the land-sale policy of the federal and state governments is well illustrated in the case of the University of Wisconsin. The select committee of the Wisconsin legislature, considering in 1870 a bill to appropriate money to the university, acknowledged that "the fund of the university [from the sale of its reserved land] is less than one-half what it ought to be, because its lands were sold cheap to encourage the settlement of the state." The state legislature, in response to political pressure from land speculators, fixed the sale price of land reserved to the university at the legal minimum price of $1.25 an acre. The land thus was sold "too soon and too cheap." The consequence of this mismanagement was not all negative, however, in that the fact of mismanagement by the state of this university resource provided eloquent and productive opportunities to successive presidents of the university and state governors to argue that the state should provide regular annual support for the university from its revenues to atone for its errors.[38]

This policy of educational reservations and grants was so tied to the public-land policy of the United States at to appear to be nothing but a subsidiary of this policy. It would remain as such until the issue of federal support of education in the older eastern states not carved out of the public lands could be raised and settled.

[38] Merle Curti and Vernon Carstensen, *The University of Wisconsin* (Madison, 1949), 1:301–10.

5. OLD STATES VERSUS NEW

·

The growing practice of federal land grants to new states provided an added focus for an already existing rivalry between old and new states. With Maryland again in the lead, the old states began to take an increasingly vigorous line in demanding equal treatment for themselves. From 1820 to 1850, Congress received many proposals designed to provide some measure of equalized assistance.

Only two of these proposals became law—John C. Calhoun's Deposit Act of 1836 and Henry Clay's Distribution–Preemption Act of 1841. The panic of 1837 forced the suspension of the first, and the rise in national tariffs quickly forced modification of important parts of the second. But all of the proposals in some measure reflected the continuing importance of the sale of public lands to the revenue system of the United States; all demonstrated a growing local interest in the rapidly increasing federal surplus; and all evidenced the new strains of the triangular sectional rivalry between North, South, and West, shown particularly in the relations between the old states and the new.

Specifically as regards assistance to education, these proposals marked the beginning of a movement to separate federal support of education from the limitations of public-land policy and indicated a growing sense of the legitimacy of federal provision for "the general welfare." In their suggested use of proceeds from the sale of land and of surplus revenues generally, the proposals also provided a necessary middle step in the progression from federal support of education with land grants to the regular support of education with tax revenues as a direct and budgeted expense of government available to all states.

Congressman John Nicholson of New York had early taken the first step in this new direction when, on December 4, 1809, he submitted the following resolution to the House:

> RESOLVED, That provision be made by law for a general national establishment of banks throughout the United States, and that the profits arising from the same, together with such surpluses of revenues as may accrue, be appropriated for the "general welfare," in the construction of public roads and canals, and the establishment of seminaries for education throughout the United States.[1]

Debate on reference of the resolution centered not on the desirability of roads, canals, or seminaries but on the constitutionality of the proposed national bank system. The charter of the Bank of the United States was about to expire, and many Jeffersonians opposed national banking. As a result the resolution never reached the committee stage and the matter died.

More widespread and direct efforts to equalize federal support of education next took the form of suggestions to make land grants for education to all states, old and new. On December 7, 1818, Congressman John Floyd of Virginia moved the adoption of what was to be the first of many similar resolutions in the Congress: "RESOLVED, That the committee on the Public Lands be instructed to inquire into the expediency of granting to each state, a tract of land, not exceeding one hundred thousand acres, for the endowment of an university in each state."[2]

Congressman George Poindexter of Mississippi delivered the report which reflected the western orientation of the committee. He reported unfavorably on the grounds that vesting universities with such large grants would impede settlement

---

[1] *Annals of Congress*, 11 Cong., 2 sess., 690.
[2] U. S., Congress, House, *Journal of the House of Representatives of the United States*, 15 Cong., 2 sess., 69.

and lower the value of the public lands near the unoccupied tracts.

The same resolution, introduced in the first session of the next Congress, was answered unfavorably by Congressman Richard C. Anderson, Jr., of Kentucky for the same committee. In his report he submitted the extreme argument that it was "inexpedient to grant any tract of land to a State for the purpose of endowing a university."[3]

The subject of public land grants for education received further public attention as a result of the actions of the state of Maryland which, consistent with its earlier position on the ceding of western lands, now urged that all states should benefit from them. On January 10, 1821, Maryland's Senator Edward Lloyd introduced the following motion: "RESOLVED, That the Committee on Public Lands be instructed to inquire into the justice and expediency of granting land for the purpose of education within the limits of the old States, corresponding with the appropriations which have been made for the same object within the limits of the new States."[4]

Senator Jessee B. Thomas of Illinois reported unfavorably for the committee. He argued that land grants were tax-exempt and that if the old states now received substantial grants from the public lands in the new states and territories, the amount of land available for settlement and taxation in the new areas would be materially decreased. Lloyd of Maryland had argued that the grants of land should be equalized so that both new and old states could share in the federal bounty. Thomas replied that the grants to the new states were not in fact grants but were rather sales based on valuable consideration received by the government in the form of the increased price which the development of the new state gave to the unsold public lands. The compact by the new states not to tax federal lands for five years after sale provided further consideration. For these reasons the committee found it inexpedient to convey lands to the extent suggested, but concluded that it was "just

3 Ibid., 16 Cong., 1 sess., 123.
4 *Annals of Congress*, 16 Cong., 2 sess., 151.

and expedient" to grant a percentage of the proceeds of the sales of public lands to a reasonable extent, on the basis of population, for support of education in the old states. However, "justice would require" making equal grants to the new states as well.[5]

Dissatisfied with the treatment they received from the Committee on Public Lands, the Maryland delegates, Lloyd in the Senate and John Nelson in the House, reworded their resolutions which they then introduced in the first session of the next Congress. They bypassed the Committee on Public Lands in each house by submitting resolutions calling for select or special committees to consider the matter of land grants to the old states. Debate and delay, however, prevented the matter from reaching the committee stage in either house.

Senator Ninian Edwards of Illinois provided the principal opposition of the new states in the Senate, speaking for nearly two hours against the resolution of Senator Lloyd. Public lands, he maintained, represented a national and not a state resource and should not be used indiscriminately for every state purpose. To make wholesale conveyances of the kind proposed would turn federal land agents into state agents and make the public land a pawn in interstate rivalries. Furthermore, this system would cut off valuable federal revenues, thereby necessitating increased federal taxation.[6]

Several more of the old states made unsuccessful attempts to secure equal treatment. Resolutions urging public land grants for the general support of education in all states were introduced in the second session of the Twenty-fourth and Twenty-fifth congresses. The language of the resolutions indicated that the old states should receive appropriations which would "correspond in a just proportion" to those received by the new states.

The last significant pre–Civil War effort to secure general land grants for education in the old states was an unsuccessful attempt to amend a bill conveying land to Iowa for railroad

[5] *Senate Document 85*, 16 Cong., 2 sess., 2.
[6] *Annals of Congress*, 17 Cong., 1 sess., 247–68.

construction. The amendment would have provided additional distributions to the old states for the purposes of education and internal improvements.[7]

The real argument between the old and new states was not over education but rather over access to the vast reservoir of federal lands for whatever purpose they might be used. The public land commissioner, after an intensive study, concluded in a report in 1880:

> The public domain of the United States has been for almost a century the target for the designs and the hopes of thousands of schemers. It has been but little understood by the mass of the people, and its real benefits but little known outside of occupants thereon. Kept in the steady grasp of able men who have been at the head of committees of the House and Senate in the Congress of the United States, it may be safely said that they have combated and driven off more than twenty thousand propositions involving grants of lands for all conceivable objects,—for starting goat-farms, dairies, voyages around the earth, trips of exploration to the Arctic regions, schools of a hundred varieties, scientific purposes— demanding thousands of acres to be sold for the benefit of their schemes.[8]

The new states maintained that they should not be obliged to share the benefits of contributions of public lands with those who had not also shared in the hardships of the frontier. Furthermore, they did not want grants made out of the public lands within their boundaries since this involved an invasion of their vaunted sovereignty. As an alternative argument the new states took the position that the federal government should convey to them title to all the public lands within their borders and in that way help to equalize their position with the older established states in the East.

Recognizing the strength of this reasoning, the old states began to develop the argument first expressed in the previously

[7] *Senate Journal*, 32 Cong., 1 sess., 279–81.
[8] *House Executive Document 47*, 46 Cong., 3 sess., pt. 4:21–22 [Report of the Public Lands Commissioner, 1880].

discussed 1821 report of Senator Thomas of Illinois—that the proceeds of the sale of the public lands should be distributed instead of the lands themselves. The first actual proposal involved the use of an education fund embodied in the resolution submitted by Congressman Phineas White of Vermont on February 12, 1823:

> RESOLVED, That the Committee of Ways and Means be instructed to inquire into the expediency of appropriating and setting apart a moiety or portion of the avails of the annual sales of the public lands, for the purpose of establishing a permanent increasing fund; the interest of which, after it shall have increased to a given sum, shall be distributed for the promotion of education in the several states, according to the principles of equal right and justice.[9]

A similar resolution introduced in the Senate in the second session of the next Congress bypassed the Committee on Public Lands and simply provided that "the Public Lands . . . be appropriated and pledged, as a permanent and perpetual fund for Education and Internal Improvement."[10] The resolution protected the interests of the old states, however, by distribution on the basis of "representation," which would have reflected their larger population.

The states disagreed as much on the propriety and method of the distribution of the proceeds of the sale of western lands as they did on distribution or cession of the lands themselves. From 1825 to 1855, Congress received no fewer than seventeen separate proposals designed to secure distribution of the proceeds of the sale of public lands for educational and other purposes.[11] Each embodied some changes designed to meet the arguments of critics or of proponents of rival uses, such as for the building of railroads.

Congressman James Strong of New York introduced the first of these proposals on December 21, 1825:

[9] *House Journal*, 17 Cong., 2 sess., 216.
[10] *Senate Document 41*, 18 Cong., 2 sess., 1.
[11] Helen A. Miller and Andrew J. Shea, *Federal Assistance for Educational Purposes* (Washington, D. C., 1963), 86–107.

RESOLVED, That the Committee on The Public Lands be instructed to inquire into the expediency of appropriating a portion of the net annual proceeds of the sales and entries of the public lands, exclusively, for the support of common schools, and of apportioning the same among the several States in proportion to the representation of each in the House of Representatives.[12]

The committee receiving the resolution reported out favorably with an appropriate bill. The report contained several interesting arguments which, while designed to justify support of the common schools, had relevance for higher education as well. As an example, the acquisition of western lands, said the report, had resulted from the common effort of all Americans and therefore all states should receive benefits from their sale. This idea served to counter the notion that only those who had endured the rigors of the frontier should benefit from these lands.

The illustration of the founding and continued support of West Point served to answer the argument that Congress had no constitutional authority to appropriate money for education. The committee report commented,

If Congress has the constitutional power (and we believe no one denies it) to establish such a school; to draw money directly from the public Treasury for its support; to pay for teaching a boy mathematics and engineering; it may be difficult to show that Congress has not the power to employ a few acres of the public domain to teach a poor man's son how to read.[13]

After citing the history of previous grants for schools, colleges, roads, and canals, the report concluded with the economic argument that only the interest of the proceeds of the sales of public lands ought to be appropriated. "As this domain is not exhaustless, if the principal, set apart for the use of these common schools, be annually expended, its benefits will be chiefly confined to our own time."

[12] *House Journal*, 19 Cong., 1 sess., 80.
[13] *House Report 88*, 19 Cong., 1 sess., 3–4.

Congressman John C. Weems of Maryland carried the argument of the old states further in submitting a resolution on January 3, 1828, designed to achieve the appropriation of public lands or a portion of the proceeds of their sale "for the advancement of common schools in the thirteen old States, equivalent to what has been granted to those States that have been introduced into the Union since the adoption of the General Government, so as to equalize the advantage of each and all the States. . . ."[14]

Recognizing the western, public-land–state orientation of the Public Lands Committee, Weems subsequently amended his resolution to refer it to a select committee. Congressman Joseph Duncan of Illinois, however, attempted to protect the interests of the new states by an amendment providing payment to them of an amount equal to the exempted tax on all the land sold or disposed of by the federal government.

Congressman Jonathan Hunt of Vermont in 1829 took the next step in the efforts of the old states by joining education and internal improvements as beneficiaries of the distribution of the proceeds, believing that the benefit to the nation from internal improvements might be more easily demonstrated. As chairman of the select committee which received his resolution, he reported favorably, although a minority within the committee submitted a separate bill. Again, constitutional arguments dominated the discussion. The committee cited the history of land grants for both education and internal improvements as having "long been considered by different administrations as the exercise of power authorized by the Constitution." The report concluded that "if Congress can make direct grants of land to literary institutions or to individual States, the power of granting the money arising from the sales, would seem to be necessarily implied."[15]

In the same Congress a new bill designed to expedite the handling of educational proposals was introduced. The conflict between old and new states had been most evident in dis-

---

[14] *House Journal*, 20 Cong., 2 sess., 153–54.
[15] *House Report 312*, 21 Cong., 1 sess., 5.

cussions of where to refer proposals for educational grants. On December 15, 1829, Congressman Joseph Richardson of Massachusetts moved that the House rules be amended by adding a "Committee on Education," which would "take into consideration all measures and propositions relative thereto, which shall be referred to them by the House, and to report their opinion thereupon, together with such propositions relative thereto, as they shall deem expedient."[16] Unfortunately, the House took no action on the matter in either session, and the idea remained dormant until 1867 when the executive branch revived it in the establishment of the Bureau of Education in the Department of the Interior.

The struggle between the new and old states became further complicated by the fact that the resolution of Senator John M. Clayton of Delaware, on March 23, 1832, was referred to the eastern-oriented and old-state-dominated Committee on Manufactures. Clayton's motion reflected the interests of the old states by providing "that the Committee on Manufactures be instructed to inquire into the expediency of distributing the public lands, or the proceeds of the sale thereof, among the several States, on equitable principles."[17]

The speech in support of his motion recalled many of the arguments of earlier resolutions that the public lands and the proceeds of their sales should benefit everyone. Clayton represented the old states in this matter. But he also represented the Whig point of view which opposed the concentration of power in executive hands and he spoke of how the distribution would "reduce the dangerous and increasing influence of the Executive patronage."

Debate of Clayton's resolution revealed the close political relationship between the support of education and internal improvements, the tariff, public lands, the surplus, and the political fortunes of men involved with these matters.[18] The

---

[16] *Senate Journal*, 22 Cong., 1 sess., 203.

[17] *Congressional Debates*, 22 Cong., 1 sess., 638.

[18] Raynor G. Wellington, *The Political and Sectional Influence of the Public Lands, 1828–1842* (New York, 1914), 38–48.

Committee of Manufactures was involved primarily because of the relation of grants for education to the tariff and the other elements of the total revenue system. Also, the Democratic administration wished to embarrass the presidential hopes of the Whig chairman of the committee, Senator Henry Clay, by placing him in the position of having to favor one section of the country over another. Thus the Senate instructed the committee "to inquire into the expediency of reducing the price of public lands, and of ceding them to the several States within which they are situated, on reasonable terms."[19] If Clay reported negatively, he would alienate the South and the West. If he decided favorably, he would alienate the East.

As a prelude to the recommendation of his report, Clay discussed the results of an exhaustive study of the public lands made by the treasury at the request of the committee. The report showed the interesting fact that, as of 1832, 227,293,-884 acres of public lands remained unsold in the ten western and southern states. Acres donated to these same states totaled 11,057,685, which included among other things only 508,-000 acres for higher education as against 7,952,538 acres for common schools and 2,187,665 acres for internal improvements.[20] In his recommendation, Clay rejected the idea of reducing the price of the public lands and instead reported a new bill entitled "A bill to appropriate, for a limited time, the proceeds of the sales of the Public Lands of the United States, and for granting lands to certain States."[21]

This bill represented another example of Clay's famous compromising skill, for it attempted to steer a middle ground between the desires of the old states, which wanted distribution of the proceeds to all the states on the basis of their population, and the new states, which wanted all the public lands ceded to the states in which they were located. SECTION 1 of the bill favored the new states by providing land for the western states over and above what they had received at the time of their ad-

[19] *Congressional Debates*, 22 Cong., 1 sess., app., 112.
[20] *Senate Document 128*, 22 Cong., 1 sess., 15.
[21] S. 179, 22 Cong., 1 sess.

mission. Section 2 favored the old states by providing that the new proceeds received after 1832 should be divided among all the states according to their respective federal representation: "To be applied by the Legislatures of the said States to such objects of education, internal improvements, colonization, or reimbursement of any existing debt contracted for internal improvements, as the said Legislatures may severally designate and authorize. . . ."

As a result of substantial pressure from Democratic Senator Thomas H. Benton of Missouri and other representatives of the new states, and over the violent objections of Senator Clay, the Senate took the extraordinary step of referring the report of the Committee on Manufactures and the Clay bill to the Committee on Public Lands for review. Chairman William R. King of Alabama reported for the latter committee and on several grounds charged Clay's report with inaccuracy. King then submitted an alternate bill proposing to decrease the price of the public lands and to make large-scale distributions of the proceeds to the western states.

The debate on the two bills continued with considerable personal acrimony through both sessions of the Twenty-second Congress. Clay's bill, amended to strike out the specific designations as to use so that there would be no tinge of federal dictation, finally passed both houses only to be killed by President Jackson's veto.[22]

Efforts to equalize support of education have thus far been discussed primarily in relation to the use of public land or the proceeds of its sale. Yet, as early as 1826, Congress received resolutions and petitions to aid education through a general distribution of surplus revenues. On January 30 of that year, Senator Mahlon Dickerson of New Jersey introduced the following resolution in the Senate:

RESOLVED, That provision ought to be made by law, to authorize and require the Secretary of the Treasury, to dis-

---

[22] James D. Richardson, ed., *A Compilation of the Messages and Papers of the Presidents 1789–1902* (Washington, D. C., 1910), 6: 1275.

tribute, annually, to the States and Territories of the United States, three millions of dollars, for the purposes of education and internal improvements, to be apportioned among the States and Territories according to the rate of direct taxation.[23]

Senator Dickerson reported favorably for the select committee which received the resolution. He argued that whether Congress used the money to reduce the national debt or distributed it as proposed was merely a question of expediency. In his mind, the distribution would have substantially beneficial results. He argued that the money would earn more in the hands of the states than the 5 percent interest rate on the national debt; that since Europeans held a large share of the debt, payment would result in a drain of money out of the country; that money distributed would stimulate local industry at the same time it relieved Congress of the task of inventing pork-barrel legislation for the disposal of the surplus; and finally, that the plan would "secure impartial justice to all the States in the distribution of expenditures of our revenue, a failure of which, at present, is a subject of loud and just complaint."[24]

The arguments in favor of the resolution must be judged to have been premature since the Senate took no action on it. Yet, these same arguments came to prevail ten years later in the Deposit Act of 1836 engineered by John C. Calhoun. The major difference in the two periods was the fact that by 1836 the federal surplus, resulting from land sales and import duties, had grown from insignificant size to approximately $25 million.

Jackson had proposed distribution of the surplus in his first annual message, but Calhoun had opposed it, regarding it mainly as a means of maintaining the hated tariff. The Compromise Tariff of 1833 provided for a lowering of the tariff, thus reducing revenues, but the increase in the sales of the public lands more than offset this reduction. By 1835 the public debt was liquidated and the surplus continued to mount.

[23] *Senate Journal*, 19 Cong., 1 sess., 118.
[24] *Senate Document 95*, 19 Cong., 1 sess., 2.

Calhoun saw in this mounting surplus the danger of vast financial patronage supporting the Jackson administration. Thus, on January 7, 1835, he offered a resolution in Congress designed to curb executive patronage.[25] A month later, when Calhoun reported out an appropriate bill from the committee which received his resolution, he also attempted to get committee support for a resolution proposing the regulation of the deposit of public money in "pet banks" and securing the passage of a constitutional amendment to legitimize the distribution of the surplus to the states.[26] With these measures, Calhoun had in view reforming the federal government, reviving the power of the states, and securing badly needed railroad funds for the South.

The committee never reported out the constitutional amendment, but after considerable debate the regulation sections of Calhoun's resolution passed both houses as Senate bill 42. On June 23, 1836, the bill received the president's signature as "An Act to Regulate the Deposits of the Public Money."[27] The act provided for the "deposit" of $35 million of the federal surplus with the states in proportion to their representation in Congress. Congress authorized the president first to deduct $5 million to provide for contingencies and then to distribute the remainder to the states subject to their agreement to pledge repayment on recall and to declare their proposed use of the funds. Although termed a loan or a deposit, the states everywhere regarded it as a gift. In all, the federal treasury distributed three installments totaling $28,101,645 to twenty-seven states before the panic of 1837 forced the suspension of the provisions of the act.

The purposes of the Deposit Act were primarily financial and reforming. However, sixteen of the twenty-seven states receiving funds under the act designated all or a portion of their receipts specifically for support of education, while the

[25] *Senate Journal*, 23 Cong., 2 sess., 79.
[26] Ibid., 148.
[27] 5 *Stat.* 52 (1836).

remainder declared that the funds be used for general purposes, which included education and internal improvements.[28]

The Deposit Act did not settle the dispute between the old and the new states regarding the disposition of public lands. Distribution had been made of the general surplus with no specific mention of the distribution of the proceeds of the sale of public lands. The South and West stood for cession of public lands to the states wherein they lay, while the North and the East favored distribution of the proceeds to all the states.

The debate continued, revived again by the Maryland congressmen. On December 22, 1838, Congressman William C. Johnson introduced a motion in the House as follows:

> RESOLVED, That a committee of one from each State be appointed by the Chair, to inquire into the propriety of reporting a bill to appropriate, for the purposes of free schools, academies, and the purposes of education, an increased portion of the public lands, for the benefit of all the States and Territories.[29]

Henry Clay had been as concerned as Calhoun with the problems of the revenue system but, with Calhoun, considered a general distribution of the surplus to be unconstitutional. Clay, however, favored going to the source of the problem, namely, the sale of public lands over which Congress had clearer constitutional authority. He also wanted to secure the proceeds of the sale of lands for internal improvements. His distribution bill had been vetoed in 1833, but he revived it again as the basis of the Distribution–Pre-emption Act of 1841.

The politics of the passage of this bill were complicated in the extreme. Both parties split into sectional factions which took different stands on the matters of tariff, graduation of the price of public lands, distribution of the proceeds of the sale of lands, cession of the lands to the states, the right of pre-

---

[28] Frank W. Blackmar, *The History of Federal and State Aid to Higher Education in the United States* (Washington, D. C., 1890), 46–47.

[29] *House Journal*, 25 Cong., 2 sess., 143.

emption, and the need for internal improvements. The problem of the surplus had been shelved by the depression of 1837, but all these other matters were in issue in the debates on Clay's distribution resolution. Finally, in order to satisfy the western Whigs, whose votes he needed, Clay was forced to support a combined distribution and pre-emption bill. As it finally became law on September 4, 1841, the bill bore the title "An Act to Appropriate the Proceeds of the Sales of the Public Lands, and to Grant Pre-emption Rights."[30]

In addition to the pre-emption features, the act contained three distribution features which embodied the concessions made to the different political sections. Firstly, the act provided a bonus of 10 percent of the proceeds of the sales of public lands for the states that contained the lands. The remainder of the proceeds after deducting certain expenses was divided among the states and territories on the basis of their federal representation.

Secondly, the act provided for the suspension of distribution when the tariff duties rose above 20 percent on any imported item, which happened soon after the passage of the act. Thus, tied to the tariff, distribution became inoperative after 1842, whereas the pre-emption section benefiting western settlers remained in effect until it was repealed in 1891.

In a third section, the western states each received grants of 500,000 acres for internal improvements. This section also extended the grant policy to all future states to be formed out of the public domain. As discussed in chapter 4, most of the states receiving the grant used a part of the acreage for support of education.

Thus the Distribution Act of 1841, together with the Deposit Act of 1836, provided victories for the East in that they represented the principal measures prior to 1862 in which all the states shared in the distribution of federal funds that could be used for educational purposes. However, since pre-emption was the western plank of the Distribution–Pre-emption Act,

---

[30] 5 *Stat.* 453 (1841).

the continued operation of pre-emption in the face of the failure of distribution represented victory of the West in the battle over public lands. The score was not evened until the eastern states succeeded in passing the Morrill Land-Grant College Act in 1862, which finally made possible distribution from public lands to all states.

In several ways the years 1820–1850 serve as a transitional period in the history of federal support of higher education. While federal assistance to education remained intimately tied to the public land policy, the first serious efforts to provide assistance from other sources occurred during this period.

The land-grant program for new states had also provided for support of both the secondary and the higher levels of education. The efforts to distribute the treasury surplus and the proceeds of the sales of public lands frequently came to distinguish between the levels of education to be supported. Increasingly from the 1820's to the 1850's, resolutions and bills in Congress constituted separate efforts to gain support either for the common schools or for higher education.

During this period, education also became increasingly separated from internal improvements as a public cause to be supported by public funds. Bills designed to achieve support of education were increasingly introduced separately from those supporting internal improvements. At the same time, education began to face growing competition from canals, toll roads, and railroads as beneficiaries of federal land-grant programs.

Perhaps most significantly, during this period the old states began their drive to achieve equality with the new states in obtaining federal support of education. The attempted use of the proceeds of the sale of public lands led naturally to considerations of the use of land scrip in the subsequent Morrill land-grant bills. It was also only a short step from the distribution of the federal surplus created in part by tax programs to the use of regular tax revenue for support of education. Thus, even though the period produced only two congressional acts providing funds which could be used for educational purposes, the climate of the congressional opinion was sufficiently molded to make possible passage of significant federal measures for support of education in the 1860's.

6. SCIENCE, POLITICS, AND

THE NEW EDUCATION

·

While congressional interest in education broadened, three major forces were at work which affected the nature of efforts to secure federal aid for education. First, the growth and public acceptance of science made new approaches to education necessary. Second, the increase in the demands of the farmer for the application of science to farming provided the impetus for the establishment of new kinds of educational institutions. Third, the emergence of the Republican party and the eclipse of the Democratic party produced the political climate in which government aid to these new institutions became politically possible. But these things were a long time in the making and the nation did not see their full effect until the passage of the Morrill Land-Grant College Act of 1862.

The rise of science predated the emergence of the other forces, aided by the fact of early government interest in support of science. Article 1, Section 8, of the Constitution granted Congress power "to promote the Progress of Science and useful Arts, by securing for limited Times to Authors and Inventors the exclusive Right to their respective Writings and Discoveries." Then in 1790, Congress passed the first patent law at the request of President Washington. By 1836 applications for patents had increased to the point that made it necessary to reorganize the federal patent office set up under the terms of the earlier act. In the twenty-three years following 1837, the number of patents granted annually increased from 436 to 4,778.[1] These were the years of the early forms

[1] A. Hunter Dupree, *Science in the Federal Government* (New York, 1957), 47.

of research and development that subsequently produced the telegraph, the reaper, and the electric motor.

The regulation and licensing of patents illustrated only one aspect of the relationship of the government to the discovery and application of scientific knowledge. In some important areas, the government actually conducted or sponsored scientific explorations and surveys. Congressional support of the explorations of Lewis and Clark, combining the interests of commerce and science, served to establish a precedent for future activities. Congress appropriated $2,500 for the expedition on the basis of the power granted in the commerce clause of the Constitution.[2] Jefferson, however, chose Captain Meriwether Lewis to lead the group because of his knowledge of "botany, natural history, minerology, and astronomy." Stephen H. Long and Zebulon Pike made their journeys of exploration under the auspices of the War Department, with each man having a scientific as well as military command.

In the early years of Jefferson's presidency, a congressional grant of $50,000 underwrote the first coastal survey. Massachusetts in 1831 became the first state to survey its natural resources. Navy and Army engineers soon followed with extensive surveys carried out under the United States Exploring Expedition, which had been established with a federal appropriation of $150,000 in 1836 in the name of assistance to commerce. During the period 1839–1842 the Wilkes Expedition to the Pacific gathered thousands of samples of seeds and plants for the newly created National Institute for the Promotion of Science. Charles Darwin in the South Pacific and James Ross in the Antarctic made research a recognized and highly respected activity. And by 1842 even John Quincy Adams's "light-house of the skies" had become a reality with the establishment of the Naval Observatory. Through the activities of the Government Land Office, Congress acted to reserve valuable mineral lands in the public domain on the basis of federally conducted surveys of government-owned land. Federally sponsored research came more and more to serve as the basis

[2] Ibid., 26.

of public policy. The first federal research contract was negotiated in 1836 when the United States government contracted with the Franklin Institute of Philadelphia to provide information necessary for realistic safety regulation of the causes of steam boiler explosions.[3]

The scientific aspects of these explorations, surveys, and experiments undertaken for the government mainly by the military required military men with more than just soldiering capabilities and training. Thus, before his journey, Meriwether Lewis went to Philadelphia to receive special instruction from the American Philosophical Society in the methods of celestial observation and collecting plants and animals, and the anthropological study of the Indians. The government recognized the need for a more permanent organization capable of providing this and other technical instruction. Consequently, in 1802, Congress established "a Corps of Engineers," stationed at West Point in New York and constituting a military academy.

This congressional action reflected the effect of the many new currents flowing into the mainstream of American education. From Europe came the influence of the work of Jean Jacques Rousseau, Johann Heinrich Pestalozzi, and Philipp Emanuel von Fellenberg, focusing on the change in emphasis from passive reception to active participation. From Europe also came the Lancastrian Plan, the Sunday school movement, manual training programs, and the kindergarten. In America the work of men like Horace Mann and Henry Barnard in the free-school movement emphasized the American ideal of education as a public responsibility supported by the state. The newly organized state public school systems represented a commitment to the cultural, social, and economic equality of the common man. The period of Jacksonian democracy also saw the introduction of the first higher educational opportunities for women when the names of Emma Willard and Mary Lyons were added to those of Mann and Barnard.

[3] *Executive Document 162*, 24 Cong., 1 sess., 1–2.

Because of these developments the classical college curriculum became increasingly inadequate to the times. Francis Wayland's report to the Brown University trustees in 1850 spelled out the situation in vivid terms. Speaking of the growing demand for engineers, he remarked that "West Point, graduating annually a smaller number than many of our colleges, has done more towards the construction of railroads than all our one hundred and twenty colleges united." He pointed out, moreover, that the proportion of college graduates to the whole population was decreasing, and commented: "We are, therefore, forced to adopt the . . . supposition that our colleges are not filled because we do not furnish the education desired by the people. . . ."[4]

Science began making inroads into the traditional centers of learning as scholars in increasing numbers traveled to Germany to learn the new methods of science and research. Chairs of chemistry appeared for the first time in 1802 at Columbia and in 1803 at Yale. In 1846, Abbott Lawrence established his scientific school at Harvard. The organization of what ultimately became the Sheffield Scientific School at Yale dated from the same year.

Education had to be practical, to be good for something. Science in the traditional colleges still resembled literature too closely in that it was to be studied but not applied. Men with vision and practical sense came to realize that new institutions were needed with practical curricula. The first of these new schools was West Point. Army engineers, trained at the military academy, provided the nation's principal source of engineers for the first half of the century.

Then Stephen Van Rensselaer, moved by a desire "to apply science to the common purposes of life," founded a new school at Troy, New York. Rensselaer Polytechnic Institute opened in 1824 with a curriculum designed "to qualify teachers for instructing the sons and daughters of farmers and mechanics, by lectures and otherwise, in the application of experimental

[4] Walter C. Bronson, *The History of Brown University, 1764–1914* (Providence, 1914), 261–62.

chemistry, philosophy, and natural history to agriculture, domestic economy, the arts, and manufactures."[5] However, the program of the institute rapidly switched to engineering, which proved to be the fastest-growing and most profitable field of the new education.

Engineering education, however, did not yet speak to the needs of the farmer, and the application of the new ideas in science and education to farming became a matter of considerable discussion. To the extent that the government had already provided assistance to the farmer, it had traditionally been in the form of cheap land, credit relaxation, and ease of entry on the land through pre-emption, graduation, and homestead laws. By the 1840's the farmer came to realize that he had other and equally serious problems besides that of the availability of cheap land. Farm land in New England was becoming exhausted with farm yields dropping to the point where the area could no longer even feed itself. Wheat rust, potato bug, and cattle disease left ravaged crops and herds that defied the normal home remedies. The decline of farm prices following the collapse of the speculative land boom in 1837 exposed many a ruined farmer as a small businessman without the protection of tariff laws, patent rights, and governmental charters that served other segments of the business community.

The farmer, however, had strength in other directions. By the 1850's no other economic group was so adequately represented by state and national societies; by local, county, and state fairs; by weekly and monthly journals; and by numerous experts who wrote regularly for newspapers and periodicals on farm problems.[6] Increasingly, these organs of farm society began to urge adoption of new scientific agriculture to reverse soil damage and to aid in fighting disease. Above all they urged governmental support of agricultural education and the dissemination of new information.

[5] Charles F. Thwing, *A History of Higher Education in America* (New York, 1909), 421.
[6] Paul Wallace Gates, *The Farmers' Age: Agriculture 1815–1860* (New York, 1960), 338.

The success of public support for the common school indicated a path to be taken, and the farmer turned first to his state government for assistance. In 1823 New York State received the first petition "looking to the establishment of a state agricultural school." In 1838 the same state received a petition with 6,000 signatures attached asking for state aid in the education of future farmers.[7]

The voice of labor did not sound as loudly on behalf of the new approach to education as did that of the farmer. In the early years of labor organizations, many groups stressed their interest in education. Workingmen's parties which appeared in many cities by the end of the 1820's demanded broad social and even utopian objectives, such as universal public education, so that the inferiorities of economic status would not automatically be passed on to their children.

The panic of 1837 and the following depression, combined with the vast new unskilled immigration, marked a watershed in the history of American labor. The emphasis of labor demands turned from long-range social and utopian measures to more job-related benefits involving wages, hours, conditions of work, and vocational training. Thus labor documents from 1840 to 1860 are not so rich in educational references as are those for the earlier period. "In the two decades preceding the Civil War, the points of contact between our educational development and organized labor were neither many nor important."[8]

To the extent to which organized labor expressed interest in education, it was in state agricultural and mechanical schools as extensions of the free common school that would provide an educational opportunity for the working farmer or mechanic. These institutions were thought to serve the interests of the working man better than would collegiate institutions or professional institutes for the training of engineers

[7] Fred A. Shannon, *The Farmers' Last Frontier: Agriculture 1860–1897* (New York, 1945), 272.
[8] Philip R. V. Curoe, *Educational Attitudes and Policies of Organized Labor in the United States* (New York, 1926), 161.

77

and scientific agriculturalists. Thus the direct and immediate initiative for change in higher education came more from educators, political leaders, and students of social and industrial matters who were apt to use the term "industrial classes" for all underprivileged, than from those concerned with the problems of the farmer.

The first institution exclusively devoted to the education of farmers and mechanics was the Gardiner Lyceum founded in Maine in 1832 to give these groups such an education as would "enable them to become skilled in their professions." The founding of the Farmers College in Ohio in 1842 and the Peoples' College in Havana, New York, in 1851 reflected similar objectives, although the farm interests were stronger than those of the mechanic. The Michigan constitution of 1850 provided in Article 13, Section 11, that: "The legislature should encourage the promotion of intellectual, scientific and agricultural improvements, and as soon as practicable provide for the establishment of an agricultural school." Michigan State Agricultural College dates its founding at Lansing from 1857. By 1860, Maryland, Massachusetts, and Pennsylvania also had colleges of agriculture.

Popular sentiment had clearly begun to shift in the direction of practical education and the practical application of theoretical training. Agricultural societies of the eastern and midwestern states began petitioning their state legislatures to establish agricultural colleges and experimental farms as well as agricultural courses in existing institutions. By 1860 the legislatures of five states—Maryland, Michigan, New York, Ohio, and Pennsylvania—had authorized the founding of such institutions and had appropriated money for their support. Meanwhile, an increasing number of existing colleges developed departments of science and agriculture.[9]

Up to this point, the only branch of the federal government specifically concerned with the farmer was the Agricultural Division of the General Patent Office. Under Patent Commis-

[9] Alfred C. True, *A History of Agricultural Education in the United States, 1785–1925* (Washington, D. C., 1929), 45–88.

sioners Henry Ellsworth, Edmund Burke, and Daniel Browne, the office served usefully to collect specimens, gather statistics, and distribute information. In 1847 the office published the findings of a special agent sent to Europe to examine the status of agricultural education. Once again Europe provided the lead, as the report showed that the governments of Russia, Prussia, France, the Netherlands, the Scandinavian countries, and Great Britain supported agricultural societies and schools of quality.

A careful review of the situation was set out in a minority report of the House Committee on Public Lands which reviewed the first Morrill bill in 1858. Congressman David Wallbridge of Michigan, author of the report, indicated that one-half of the free male population of the United States over fifteen years of age (by the census of 1850) was directly engaged in farming. Yet, he said, this large part of the population was "notoriously less instructed in those branches of scientific knowledge directly connected with the proper and economic management of their own pursuits than any other class of citizens. . . ." He commented further that the free male population over fifteen numbered 5,371,876, of whom 2,389,013 were farmers, compared with 94,515 members of the learned professions of law, medicine, and divinity. These latter had 234 colleges, with millions in endowment to serve them, but the farmer had only a handful of institutions, meagerly supported. Agricultural products grossed $1,500 million annually, compared with $650 million for foreign commerce. Yet, the government spent millions on the Navy, naval schools, lighthouses, coastal surveys, and harbor improvements.[10]

Aid from state governments provided local assistance, but increasing agitation developed for a national approach to the problems of agricultural education. As early as February 3, 1840, Congress received a memorial calling for the establishment of a national Department of Agriculture and Education.[11] The first definite proposal made to Congress to provide

[10] *House Report 261*, 35 Cong., 1 sess., 6–14.
[11] *Senate Document 181*, 26 Cong., 1 sess., 2.

large-scale aid to each state for new education came from Captain Allen Partridge of Vermont on January 21, 1841. His plan called for an appropriation of $40 million from the proceeds of the sale of public lands to be paid to the states in annual installments on the basis of representation in the House of Representatives. Each state could use the money to establish a new institution or remodel an existing one which would offer a broad curriculum of natural and economic sciences with application to agriculture, engineering, manufacturing, and commerce, as well as to military science.[12]

In 1853 the Massachusetts legislature petitioned Congress for the establishment of "a national normal agricultural college," endowed with public lands, "to be to the rural sciences, what West Point is to the military. . . ."[13] More important, because of the eventual adoption of its principle, was the resolution received by Congress on March 20, 1854, from the Illinois legislature. This document urged passage of an act "donating to each State in the Union an amount of public lands not less in value than five hundred thousand dollars for the liberal endowment of a system of industrial universities—one in each State in the Union. . . ."[14]

This resolution reflected the work in Illinois of Jonathan Baldwin Turner, considered by some as the real father of the Land-Grant College Act of 1862.[15] The dispute about the authorship of that measure is not of concern here, as the significance of Turner's activity in the 1850's is clear in any case. He received great publicity in 1850 and 1851 for his "plan for an Industrial University for Illinois," unveiled first at agricultural and industrial conventions around the state. The plan then received great notice when reprinted in the widely read journal *The Prairie Farmer* and in the 1851 report of the

---

[12] *Executive Document 69*, 26 Cong., 2 sess., 6.

[13] *Acts and Resolves of Massachusetts* (1852), 285.

[14] *House Miscellaneous Report 31*, 33 Cong., 1 sess., 1–2.

[15] Edmund J. James, "The Origin of the Land-Grant Act of 1862 and Some Account of its Author, Jonathan B. Turner," *University of Illinois Studies*, 4, no. 1 (Urbana, Ill., 1910).

United States Commissioner of Patents. His plan then became the basis of the Illinois proposal discussed above.

Federal aid in the form of land grants clearly offered the best means of assisting the new educational institutions desired by farm, industrial, and reform interests. Few constitutional scruples remained against the use of public lands or proceeds from their sale in 1850 except among Southerners.[16] Money grants from general Treasury funds, however, had not yet found constitutional acceptance. In arguing for his distribution bill in 1841, Henry Clay had distinguished between the constitutionality of grants of land (or proceeds from land sales) and the use of general funds. He said:

> I wish to guard against all misconception by repeating,
> what I have heretofore several times said, that this bill is
> not founded upon any notion of a power in Congress to lay
> and collect taxes, and distribute the amount among the
> several States. I think Congress possesses no such power, and
> has no right to exercise it until some amendment as that pro-
> posed by the Senator from South Carolina (Mr. Calhoun)
> shall be adopted. But the bill rests on the basis of a clear
> and comprehensive grant of power to Congress over the
> Territories and property of the United States in the constitu-
> tion, and upon express stipulations in the deeds of cession.[17]

Arguments about the use of public land continued as the eastern states maintained their conviction that all states had the right to share in the benefits derived from public land. These eastern states, consequently, were not enthusiastic about the federal programs of land donations through subsidies, bounties, pre-emption, graduation, and homestead laws, all of which favored the western states.

The sectional rivalry over the public lands question had three dimensions, with the East and the Middle West in favor of distribution of land or the proceeds of the sale of the lands to all states, the South favoring cession of the lands to the

---

[16] Gates, *The Farmers' Age*, 374.
[17] *Congressional Debates*, 24 Cong., 1 sess., 50.

states wherein they lay, and the West favoring both cession and a liberal policy of grants to individuals. In addition, the major political parties had traditionally taken opposing views on the public lands question. From the time of President Jackson, the Democrats had been the party of strict construction of the Constitution and of limited government. Jackson's vetoes of the Maysville road bill and the first distribution bill, and his destruction of the National Bank, helped set the tone of Democratic political theory which prevailed until the Civil War.

These principles of limited government appeared as specific planks in the Democratic party platforms from 1840 to 1856. Section 1 of the 1840 platform read as follows: "RESOLVED, That the federal government is one of limited powers, derived solely from the constitution, and the grants of power shown therein ought to be strictly construed by all the departments and agents of the government, and that it is inexpedient and dangerous to exercise doubtful constitutional powers."[18] Sections 2 and 3 specifically denied that Congress had the power to conduct a general program of internal improvements, or to favor one section of the country or branch of industry over any other. The 1844 platform then included the following specific plank on the public lands question which remained in the party platform until 1856: "RESOLVED, That the proceeds of the Public Lands ought to be sacredly applied to the national objects specified in the Constitution, and that we are opposed to the laws lately adopted, and to any law for the Distribution of such proceeds among the States, as alike inexpedient in policy and repugnant to the Constitution."

By contrast, the Whig platform of 1844 came out specifically in favor of distribution of the proceeds from sale of public lands. While the Republican platforms of 1856 and 1860 contained no specific mention of the public lands, it remained clear that the Whig and Republican parties had fundamentally different positions on the question of the powers of the

[18] Kirk H. Porter and Donald Bruce Johnson, eds., *National Party Platforms, 1840–1964* (Urbana, Ill., 1966), 2.

federal government from those of the Democratic party. Individual party members might differ among themselves with, for example, many Democrats favoring internal improvements, tariffs, and the like, but the official differences remained.

The Democratic party position came into sharp focus during the Pierce administration. Elements of the reform movement of the 1830's and 1840's joined forces with representatives of the eastern states anxious to secure an increased share of the benefits of the public lands. A congressional bill resulted, sponsored by Dorothea Dix of Massachusetts and introduced in the House by Congressman Solomon Foot of Vermont, "making a grant of public lands to the several states and territories of the Union for the benefit of the indigent insane persons."[19] The bill would have appropriated 10 million acres to be apportioned among the states in the compound ratio of geographic area and representation in the House. As amended, it contained the provision that states with no public land would receive scrip representing lands available elsewhere.

Congress had acted previously to grant land in support of institutions somewhat similar to those proposed in the Dix-Foot bill. On March 3, 1819, the Connecticut Asylum for the Deaf and Dumb at Hartford received a congressional grant of land.[20] On the basis of the argument that it was the only such institution in the West, the Kentucky Asylum for the Deaf and Dumb also received a grant of land on April 5, 1826.[21]

Along with the Dix-Foot bill, Congress also considered the Turner Plan as presented by the Illinois petition. The Turner Plan called for equal grants of money from the sale of public lands to each state as against the provision of the Dix-Foot bill, appropriating land on the basis of population and size. The Turner Plan never emerged from committee. After considerable discussion, the Dix-Foot bill passed both houses only

[19] U. S., Congress, *The Congressional Globe*, 33 Cong., 1 sess., 73–74.
[20] 6 *Stat.* 229 (1819).
[21] Ibid., 339.

to be vetoed by the Democratic President Pierce on May 3, 1854.[22]

In his veto message, President Pierce repudiated the Connecticut and Kentucky precedents by saying that Congress had acted in error in granting the aid. Care of the insane was a local state matter, and if Congress could properly assume responsibility for the care of the insane, it could also care for the sane and thus take over all the domestic duties of the states, making a mockery out of the Constitution. Any federal grant to support a local institution was clearly unconstitutional, Pierce declared. He could not find "any authority in the Constitution for making the Federal Government the great almoner of public charity throughout the United States." The message left no doubt about what the president would do with a bill granting land for educational or any other public welfare purpose.

Such was the background when on February 28, 1856, Justin S. Morrill, a freshman Republican congressman from Vermont, called for the establishment of "one or more national agricultural schools upon the basis of the naval and military schools, in order that one scholar from each congressional district, and two from each State at large, may receive a scientific and practical education at the public expense."[23]

Southern Democratic opposition prevented any further action on the matter, but an important and historic step had been taken. Morrill did not become discouraged easily, and on December 8, 1857, he served notice of his intention to introduce his own bill "donating public lands to the Several States and Territories which may provide colleges for the benefit of agriculture and mechanical arts."[24]

[22] James D. Richardson, ed., *Messages and Papers of the Presidents* 4:2780–89.
[23] *Congressional Globe*, 34 Cong., 1 sess., 530.
[24] *House Journal*, 35 Cong., 1 sess., 17.

7. THE LAND-GRANT COLLEGE
ACT OF 1862

·

O n December 14, 1857, Congressman Justin S. Morrill brought forward his first land-grant college bill (H. R. 2), which appropriated 20,000 acres of public lands to each state and territory for every senator and congressman to which it was entitled under the 1850 census. For the states without public lands, the bill provided for the issuance of scrip for an equal amount of land in unoccupied areas of the public-land states. This land was to provide

> the endowment, support, and maintenance of at least one college in each state where the leading object shall be, without excluding other scientific or classical studies, to teach such branches of learning as are related to agriculture and the mechanical arts as the legislatures of the states may respectively prescribe, in order to promote the liberal and practical education of the industrial classes in the several pursuits and professions of life.

Under the rules of the House this bill would normally have gone to the Committee on Public Lands. Morrill, however, attempted to secure its referral to the Committee on Agriculture, of which he was a member. He said, "I appeal to the common *fairness* of the House, to allow this subject to go to a committee where it shall not be strangled—to a committee that will be likely to mature and perfect the bill—a committee of its friends."[1]

The House would not agree and the bill went to the Committee on Public Lands. Four months later, on April 15, 1858,

---

[1] *Congressional Globe*, 35 Cong., 1 sess., 36.

Congressman William Cobb of Alabama reported back the bill with the strongest recommendation that it not pass, branding it as unconstitutional and inexpedient. Congressman David Wallbridge of Michigan, however, delivered a minority report in favor of the bill. The two reports covered the basic arguments pro and con on the merits of the bill.[2]

As a southern Democrat, Cobb objected principally to the legal incompetence of the federal government to do anything where its powers had not been specifically delegated by the Constitution. He demurred to the merits of the need to do something for the farmer but held the method to be "unconstitutional and inexpedient." He claimed that Congress had no power to appropriate common revenues, either land or money, for the support of any local, domestic, state interest. Moreover, Congress had a specific responsibility to preserve the public lands as a major source of revenue for future generations. He concluded his remarks with the statement "that Congress, without a promise of pecuniary compensation, has no power to grant portions of the public domain; and if it had, no policy could be more unwise than to grant it for the support of local institutions within the States."

Wallbridge, for the minority, also spoke to the constitutional issues involved. He listed the uses for which Congress had made appropriations of public lands, all of which, he maintained, benefited all the states. Other kinds of benefit existed beyond that of increasing the value of the remaining lands, he said. In conclusion, his report stated, "there is no limit to the uses and purposes to which the public domain may be applied but the discretion of Congress. If a proposed grant is for the benefit of all the States, Congress has full power to make it. . . ."

Morrill spoke in support of his measure and began by pointing out to his colleagues that the bill had induced a "stream

[2] U. S., Congress, House, Report from the Committee on Public Lands, *Lands for Agricultural Colleges, &c.: Report to Accompany H. R. 2*, 35 Cong., 1 sess., 1858, H. Rept. 261; Ibid., *Clerks in Land Offices in Oregon Territory: Report to Accompany H. R. 169*, 35 Cong., 1 sess., 1858, H. Rept. 262.

of petitions" in support of its passage. Congress, he said, had already legislated on behalf of most other classes of the community except the farmer. Federal aid to agriculture was desperately needed if the dire consequences of defective cultivation were to be prevented and soil losses reversed. Finally, he could see no constitutional objection to the bill, since Congress had "power to dispose of and make all needful rules and regulations respecting the territory or other property belonging to the United States."

Morrill, however, did not rely on logic and eloquence alone to secure passage of the bill. At the end of his remarks, he offered an amendment, striking out everything after the title of the original bill and substituting a new measure, which deleted all references to territories and, as an incentive, provided for a double quantity of acreage in cases where the value of the lands neighboring railroad grants raised land values to double the minimum price. Then, in a rather complicated but skillful maneuver, he introduced a parliamentary motion which had the effect of cutting off debate on the question. Over the strenuous objections of Congressman John McQueen of South Carolina that the new bill had not been considered by any committee, Morrill moved the question and brought his new bill to a vote. The House passed the amended measure on April 22 by the narrow margin of 105 to 100, with the yea's being composed mainly of free, northern, Republican votes, and the nay's of southern, slave, Democratic votes. With party allegiance following sectional lines, the vote split on a North-South axis.[3]

The bill went to the Senate the same day it passed the House, and Senator Benjamin F. Wade of Ohio undertook to guide its progress. The public lands committee received the bill in due course; and on May 6, Senator Charles Stuart of Michigan reported it back without recommendation, there being a divided vote in the committee. With Clement Clay of Alabama as their spokesman, the southern Democratic sena-

---

[3] *Congressional Globe*, 35 Cong., 1 sess., 1742.

tors took the position that the bill should not pass since the Democratic party had been on record against such a measure for many years. Sensing that they had a real fight on their hands, the supporters of the bill did not press for special consideration, and as a consequence the measure did not reappear on the floor until Congress convened for the next session in December.

There, after southern senators voiced strong opposition to the measure, the bill was returned to the Committee on Public Lands on the theory that it had never received the vote of the majority. The committee subsequently reported it back with a group of amendments designed to change the focus of the bill. This revision was to be made by eliminating Section 5, which contained some restrictions on the grants, by apportioning the land on the compound formula of the Dix-Foot bill, by tying the operation of the grant to the tariff as had been done with the Distribution–Pre-emption Act of 1841, and by eliminating some of the landed states from the provisions of the act to preserve their land from the scrip claims of the landless states. Curiously, the only amendment to pass was that striking the requirement of making annual reports to the Agricultural Division of the Patent Office, the only federal office traditionally concerned with support of agricultural programs.

The Senate passed the bill on February 7, 1859, by the close vote of 25 to 22. The House approved the Senate amendments on February 17, and the bill went to President Buchanan for his signature the next day.

Congressional opinion had divided sharply on the measure, with the principal opposition coming largely from the West and the rural South. Senator Clement Clay regarded the bill "as one of the most monstrous, iniquitous, and dangerous measures which have ever been submitted to Congress."[4] The constitutional issue posed the greatest threat to Southerners who, by 1859, were put off by any idea contrary to the doctrine of states' rights or by any attempted federal influence on local institutions. Clay even went so far as to read President

4 Ibid., 2 sess., 786.

Pierce's 1854 veto message of the Dix-Foot bill into the record in support of his opposition to the Morrill bill. On these constitutional grounds alone, the South opposed the bill almost unanimously.

As a second basis of objection the South opposed distribution of public land, favoring, rather, cession to the states wherein it lay. The South asserted it had not received an equal share of benefit from public lands, particularly considering the large amount of land its states had relinquished to the federal government. Virginia claimed not to have received a penny of the more than $79 million realized by 1849 from the sale of land in the Old Northwest. The same was true to a lesser extent for Georgia and the Carolinas as regards land in the Old Southwest. Of railroad grants by 1854, the South had received 9.3 acres per square mile to 18.5 acres for the North. Educational grants compared at 27.7 acres for the South to 38.9 acres for the North.[5]

A third basis of southern opposition was the fact that the bill made no adequate distinction between the work done by slave and overseer when it spoke of agricultural education. Both functions tended to be combined in the work of the small landowner or even the tenant farmer of the North and West. Yet, few Southerners were likely to support a measure providing education for the farmer if this could be construed to mean educating the Negro slave as well.

Western opposition developed from the fear of the speculative effect which increased absentee landowning would have on the price of land. Moreover, since the grants were based on population, many Westerners saw the act as little more than Henry Clay's distribution scheme in a new dress.[6]

In general, then, the free, northern, Republican and Whig, landless states supported the measure, while the southern, slaveowning, landed, and Democratic states opposed it. The

[5] Roy M. Robbins, *Our Landed Heritage: The Public Domain, 1776–1936* (New York, 1950), 173–74.
[6] Paul Wallace Gates, "Western Opposition to the Agricultural College Act," *Indiana Magazine of History* 38 (1941):112–14.

western vote split along party and sectional lines. Thus debate on the act tended to ignore educational questions and revolve around constitutional, states' rights, and public-land arguments. It was on these grounds that President Buchanan rested his resounding veto of the act when it came to him.[7]

The president considered the act both "inexpedient and unconstitutional." The argument of inexpediency emphasized the fact that the federal treasury was low. All the land granted would be forced onto the market at about the same time, depressing the price of public land generally and thus reducing government revenue. Further, speculators would inhibit the development and growth of new states. The new colleges founded under the terms of the act would likewise inhibit the progress of established institutions.

Principally, however, the president considered the act unconstitutional for all the reasons that Southern states' righters had reiterated since the time of Jackson. The fact that Buchanan vetoed the Morrill Act in the same year that Charles Darwin published his *Origin of Species* illustrates how completely the conservative, southern wing had come to dominate the Democratic party and shows perhaps in caricature the relationship between the forces opposing each other in the debates on the Land-Grant College Act.

Morrill came storming back, indignant at this presidential action, ignoring the fact that his bill had passed both houses with slim majorities and without the approval of either public lands committee. He had said earlier, "I know very well that when there is a lack of arguments to be brought against the merits of a measure, the Constitution is fled to as an inexaustible arsenal of supply."[8] He dismissed the constitutional arguments in opposition to the bill by asking, if grants of land to the public-land states were constitutional, how could grants be unconstitutional merely because they were to non-public-land states? Yet Morrill lacked the political strength to secure the necessary votes to override the veto. And so it stood until

[7] *Congressional Globe*, 35 Cong., 2 sess., 1412–13.
[8] Ibid., 1 sess., 1692.

a change of administration and the secession of the southern states altered the balance of political power.

Morrill introduced his bill again as H. R. 6 in the first session of the Thirty-sixth Congress on February 15, 1860. Again the western-oriented public lands committee proved the principal obstacle, reporting the measure unfavorably. Sectional loyalties again proved stronger than those of party in this issue. This fact helps explain Morrill's subsequent failure to get his bill H. R. 138 out of the public lands committee of the Republican Thirty-seventh Congress, and also explains some of the scattered northern Democratic votes for the first Morrill bill.[9]

On December 9, 1861, shortly after the Thirty-seventh Congress convened in regular session, Morrill served notice of his intention to introduce a bill "donating lands to such States and Territories as shall establish colleges for the benefit of agriculture and mechanic arts." Morrill brought forward his new bill on December 16, under the title H. R. 138, in which he made several significant changes from his earlier measures.[10] Both his earlier bills, H. R. 2 and H. R. 6, provided for grants to both states and territories of 20,000 acres for each senator and congressman. The new bill deleted the grants to territories except in the bill title and increased the basic amount to 30,000 acres. It also specifically excluded the southern states in rebellion and added the required teaching of military tactics. With the mounting casualties of the first battle of Bull Run, Shiloh, and Pea Ridge, and with McClellan in the midst of the carnage of the Peninsula campaign, the North realized that it needed trained soldiers.

The bill was referred to the Committee on Public Lands, where Chairman John E. Potter of Wisconsin reported it out unfavorably on May 29.[11] Midwestern opposition in the committee prevented Morrill from getting his bill out on the floor for debate. Again sectional loyalties outweighed those of party.

---

9 *House Journal*, 36 Cong., 1 sess., 467.
10 Ibid., 37 Cong., 2 sess., 74.
11 Ibid., 773.

With his own bill blocked in committee, Morrill's only hope of preventing the defeat of his measure was to secure the introduction of an identical bill in the Senate. Once passed by the Senate, this bill could be referred to the House, bypassing the Committee on Public Lands. Consequently, Morrill urged Senator Wade to introduce S. 298 on May 5. The bill went to the Senate public lands committee and was reported back favorably by Senator James Harlan of Iowa, with amendments, on May 16.[12] Opposition came primarily from the West, for which section Senator James H. Lane of Kansas served as the principal spokesman. The Senate voted down the committee amendments but Lane finally secured two changes in the bill. The first limited the amount of land to be selected in any of the landed states to 1 million acres so that no state would be deprived of all the best of its public lands. The second delayed the opening date for entries under the act until a year from its passage so that settlers under the newly passed Homestead Act would have the first choice of land.

With these relatively moderate changes accepted by Wade, and with his forceful leadership of the radical wing of the Republican party, the bill passed the Senate on June 10 by a vote of 32 to 9 and went to the House.[13] The House passed the bill on June 19 by a vote of 90 to 25, and on July 2, 1862, President Lincoln signed it into law.[14]

The act spelled out very carefully the limitations to the grants imposed by the federal government and the conditions involved in their acceptance by the individual states. Congress granted 30,000 acres for every senator and congressman under the 1860 census, but mineral lands were specifically excluded. No state could acquire title to lands in another state through use of scrip but had to sell the scrip to a third party. Even then, no more than 1 million acres could be located in

[12] *Senate Journal*, 37 Cong., 2 sess., 444, 496.
[13] Since it was in fact Wade's Senate bill which became law, it is more accurate to refer to the act as the Morrill-Wade Act even though it is traditionally known simply as the Morrill Act.
[14] 12 *Stat.* 503 (1862).

any one state, and a year had to elapse before any land could be located.

The act further required the states to assume all expenses relating to the selection and sale of lands, and to the management and disbursement of funds, so that the entire federal donation would be preserved as an endowment. All money realized from the sale of land or scrip was required to be invested in federal bonds or other "safe securities" and remain unimpaired as permanent funds for the endowment and support of appropriate colleges. These colleges were required to teach agriculture, mechanical arts, and military tactics, without excluding the other scientific or classical subjects.

The states were required to contribute to the maintenance of the land-grant institutions as well as to provide their buildings. None of the endowment fund could be used for buildings and only 10 percent for land for building sites. To secure the benefit of the act, a state had to signify its acceptance of the terms of the act by legislative action within two years of July 2, 1862, and then establish the required institution within five years. Each governor was required to submit annual reports to Congress on the sale of lands or scrip and the investment of the proceeds. The colleges also had to submit annual reports on their progress and expenditures to each of the other land-grant institutions and to the secretary of the interior.

As Earle Ross pointed out, the lack of great public enthusiasm for the Morrill-Wade Act, considering its enormous impact, is one of the ironies of history. Lincoln signed it without comment on its merits. Even Horace Greeley, one of the chief supporters of the measure, declared he would be satisfied if only five schools were founded under its terms.[15]

Enthusiasm did exist for the passage of the bill even if not in proportion to the significance of the measure. First, and most important, the bill appealed to the Republican politicians of the landless eastern states. The Thirty-seventh Congress had already passed the Homestead Act which, together with

[15] Earle D. Ross, *Democracy's College: The Land-Grant Movement in the Formative Stage* (Ames, Iowa, 1942), 66–67.

the federal grants at the time of admission, clearly benefited the western settlers and the new states and reflected their growing political influence. The Morrill-Wade Act provided a national system for the distribution of public lands which, as based on congressional representation, favored the old eastern states with small area and large population. A strong reason for its passage appeared to have been the desire to balance the diverse elements of the Republican party—the eastern and the western, the industrial and the agrarian—and the landed states and the landless.[16]

Further, the Morrill-Wade Act could be counted on to capture those congressional votes which were not necessarily sympathetic with the antislavery base of the Republican party but which were not attracted by the anticentralism of the Democrats. Several of the amendments to the bill reflected the desire to harmonize the divergent land policies inherent in the Morrill-Wade and Homestead acts. These delayed the date of entry under Morrill-Wade to allow settlers first entry and limited scrip to previously offered land.

The issue of the first Morrill bill had been fought out on constitutional grounds between the North and South. Whatever the debate on the merits, the issue in the second was fought out on the public-land issue between the East and the West. After losing the earlier rounds of the battle, as illustrated in the Distribution—Pre-emption Act of 1841, the eastern states won a signal political victory in 1862.

Eastern Republican votes alone could not have secured the passage of the act, and the eastern politicians realized they had strong arguments in their appeal to the farmer. It may be true, as Frederick Rudolph suggested, that the activities leading up to the Morrill-Wade Act had little to do with the pressure from farmers and workingmen's associations but was rather the work of middle-class reformers who advanced "theoretical and

[16] John Y. Simon, "The Politics of the Morrill Act," *Agricultural History* 37 (1963):109.

ideological notions of what popular technical education ought to be."[17] In 1860 the farmers had no organized agrarian program such as emerged later in the Populist movement. But the farmer could not be ignored politically; and in the still rurally dominated America of the 1850's and 1860's, appeals to the farmer had significant political pulling power, as the establishment of the United States Department of Agriculture in 1862 attests. Later, when Morrill recalled his reasons for introducing his bill, they were strongly flavored with the need and the desirability of doing something for the farmer.

Morrill also gave credit to the assistance he received from a group of interested educators. These included President Amos Brown of the Peoples' College in New York, President Joseph Williams of the Michigan Agricultural College, President John Kennecott of the Illinois Normal University, D. P. Calloway of Indiana, and M. P. Welder of Massachusetts.[18] The educational significance of the Morrill legislation arose primarily because of the subsequent importance of the institutions founded. Yet, as mentioned, the educational aspects of the measure received scant attention in the congressional debates in 1862. The passage of the act reflected concern for political strategy more than advancement of education. Nevertheless, it is interesting that Morrill and his Republican colleagues thought political necessity could best be served by making liberal grants of land to support higher education designed to benefit a particularly powerful political group. One writer even goes so far as to suggest that Morrill was anxious to obtain passage of an act benefiting the farmers so they would not object so vigorously to his 1861 tariff measure, which benefited eastern manufacturers.[19]

[17] Frederick Rudolph, *The American College and University* (New York, 1962), 249.
[18] True, *Agricultural Education*, 103.
[19] I. L. Kandel, *Federal Aid for Vocational Education*, Carnegie Foundation for the Advancement of Teaching, *Bulletin No. 10* (New York, 1917), 86–87.

Though the questions of motive and intention are open to considerable speculation, there is little question that the passage of the 1862 act constituted a major departure from previous federal practice. Land grants specifically directed to the support of higher education were given to all states on a nationwide basis for the first time. Congress imposed specific conditions on the manner of selection and sale of the lands granted as well as on the reinvestment and use of the funds realized. A definite pattern reflecting need based on population replaced the diffuse bases of the earlier grants. By directing the grants to the support of technical education, Congress forced education to fit the changing social and economic patterns of an expanding nation. The grants also gave a great boost to publicly supported education at all levels. Although there was no enforcement procedure established, a new pattern of obligations assumed by the accepting states arose to replace the almost complete lack of conditions associated with previous grants. The 1862 act also established the practice of annual reporting and accounting of federal funds about which today's educators often complain. Finally, in order to be eligible for a grant, the states had to pass legislation pledging acceptance of the terms. In combination, these features represent the beginning of a pattern which has characterized much of federal aid to education.

The act also had a significant impact judging by the number and kind of institutions it fostered. The term "land-grant college" (or university) is applied to any institution of higher education that has been recognized and designated by its state legislature as being qualified to fulfill the provisions and receive the benefits of the 1862 act and its amendments. There are now sixty-eight such institutions.[20] According to the 1960 Office of Education census they represented 3.4 percent of all the institutions of higher education in the United States, grant-

---

[20] From 1929, when Alaska Agricultural College and School of Mines was designated a land-grant institution, to 1957, when West Virginia State College went out of operation, there were sixty-nine institutions.

ing 20 percent of the master's degrees and 40 percent of the doctorates.[21]

All of these institutions are now public except Cornell and MIT, which share the land-grant funds with other colleges in their states. Some states created new institutions to take advantage of the act's provisions. Others designated already existing institutions as beneficiaries. But whatever their origin, all these colleges and universities have served the cause of education by making science, experimentation, and the laboratory method respected elements of the college curriculum. By 1927, for example, the land-grant institutions were educating almost half of the nation's engineers.

The Morrill-Wade Land-Grant Act stressed equally agriculture and mechanical arts. It was also clear that the act intended engineering in its many branches to be coordinate with agriculture as a required part of the program of land-grant institutions. The degree of support for "mechanic arts" in any single institution, however, was controlled by local need, and local legislation on the subject of land-grant institutions was for many years more beneficial to agriculture than to mechanical arts.[22]

In summary, it can be said that the Morrill-Wade Land-Grant College Act resembled the Ohio Company Contract of 1787 in many significant ways. Both were closely involved with the public-land policy and the desire for a share of the federal land. Zeal for land outweighed that for education in both cases. The significance of neither legislative act was realized at the time of its adoption, yet both established new patterns of federal aid which had great importance in the history of American education.

[21] Henry S. Brunner, *Land-Grant Colleges and Universities, 1862–1962*, United States Office of Education, *Bulletin No. 13* (Washington, D. C., 1962), 43–45.

[22] Arthur Jay Klein, ed., *Survey of Land-Grant Colleges and Universities*, United States Office of Education, *Bulletin No. 9* (Washington, D. C., 1930), I, 789–801.

8. FURTHER AID FOR

INSTRUCTION

.

The Morrill-Wade Act of 1862 granted land or scrip to the states, but each state individually had to accept the grant within two years before it became operative. Iowa, Vermont, and Connecticut acted within one year, and fourteen more states secured the benefits of the act before the end of 1864. However, the problems of biennial legislative meetings and the dislocation caused by the Civil War made it apparent that the time limit of the act would have to be extended if all the states were to be included. This extension was particularly necessary for the southern states, which were not eligible to comply with the terms until after at least the termination of the war in 1865.

On December 15, 1863, Senator Thomas Hendricks of Indiana introduced the first bill to amend the Morrill-Wade Act of 1862. As passed by both houses and signed by President Lincoln, bill S. 12 extended the time for acceptance for two years, to April 14, 1866. The bill also extended the benefits of the land-grant legislation to the newly created state of West Virginia.[1] Three states in 1864 and one in 1865 acted to accept the grant. By January 1, 1866, only Nevada, Missouri, Delaware, and the southern states were outside its provisions.

On December 18, 1865, Congressman Michael Kerr of Indiana submitted H. R. 50 to amend further Section 5 of the act by extending the period for the declaration of intent for five years and the period for compliance for ten years. The bill was

[1] 13 *Stat.* 47 (1864).

referred to the Committee on Agriculture, and within one month, Congressman John Bidwell of California reported it back with the following amendment: "That in extending the provisions of this act to the States lately in rebellion, it shall be on the express condition that no person shall be excluded on account of race or color from the benefits of the school or educational fund arising from the lands thus donated."[2]

After the initial debate on the amendment had demonstrated that a number of congressmen felt the provision on Negro rights was premature, Bidwell moved to return the bill to his committee. On March 21, 1866, he reported it out a second time, with a substitute amendment which extended the provisions of the original act to territories as well as states. This amendment met opposition on the ground that it was unreasonable for Congress to expect a sparsely populated territory to provide for a college. Bidwell moved to recommit his bill. It was reported a third time, only to be recommitted again. Finally, the measure passed both houses and received President Johnson's signature. As law, the act extended the two-year acceptance provisions of the 1862 act for three years. The act also extended the benefits to the territories when they became states.[3] By a third amendment, Congress subsequently extended the time for compliance to July 1, 1874.[4] With the benefit of these extensions, thirty-seven states, including all the southern states, had accepted the terms of the act by 1870 and had agreed to organize the appropriate colleges.

Further efforts to satisfy local conditions required additional procedural amendments of the original act. Concern for the safety and permanence of the endowment funds dictated the inclusion of the original provision that 90 percent of the money derived from the sale of land or scrip be invested as a permanent fund in government bonds, either federal or state, or in other safe securities bearing not less than 5 percent interest. The states were further required to replace all losses from the

[2] *Congressional Globe*, 39 Cong., 1 sess., 299.
[3] 14 *Stat.* 208 (1866).
[4] 17 *Stat.* 416 (1873).

endowment fund. However, in 1882, Congress authorized the state of Iowa, without forfeiture, to loan the fund on real estate security.[5] Then, by statutory amendment in 1883, Congress permitted states having no state bonds to invest the endowment fund in any manner approved by the respective state legislatures as long as the fund maintained a 5 percent income return.[6]

The attempt to allow the provisions of the Morrill-Wade Act to apply to local conditions led to a general assault on the underlying objectives of the act. During the debate on the 1864 amendment, Congressman William Holman of Indiana proposed an additional amendment whereby the states would individually determine whether they would apply the funds to education in agriculture and mechanical arts or to some other such purposes as their respective legislatures might designate. Holman had in mind the free common school education of war orphans, but the thrust of his amendment was to establish local control of the endowment fund for any purpose. Morrill responded with the comment: "As I understand it, the object of the original donation was to enable the industrial classes of the country to obtain a cheap, solid, and substantial education. I trust the House will not begin thus early to fritter away the whole purpose of that act."[7] Congressman Thaddeus Stevens of Pennsylvania supported Morrill in emphasizing the national character of his act. As he said, "When the original bill was framed it was intended to be national and to establish a national system of education, bestowing national property for that purpose."

Holman's amendment did not pass and Congress maintained the federal control of the uses of the endowment as originally provided. Holman's principle, however, survived in a limited form when, in 1866, Congress extended the benefits of the act to Nevada. In so doing, it allowed that state, without forfeiture, to divert the endowment fund from the support of

[5] 22 *Stat.* 50 (1882).
[6] 22 *Stat.* 484 (1883).
[7] *Congressional Globe*, 38 Cong., 1 sess., 1284.

teaching of agriculture and mechanical arts to that of the theory and practice of mining.[8]

Morrill struck an interesting note in the remarks quoted above in his exclusive reference to "the industrial classes" and the omission of any mention of the farmer. It would appear from this and other comments that Morrill had no fixed idea of the kind of institutions he wanted to develop, and further that he changed his concept of the groups he wished to benefit. During the debate on the original bill, Morrill stressed the need to do something for the farmer. Yet, on a visit to Yale in 1867, in a conversation summarized by a faculty member in attendance, he indicated that "he wished the bill to be broad enough so that the several states might use it to the best advantage." Though the details might vary according to the local conditions, "all the colleges should be the same in spirit and of the same grade, that is *colleges*, in which science and not classics should be the leading idea."

Leaving possible political motives aside and focusing only on what he intended to accomplish through the bill, one sees that Morrill did not present a demand for a particular kind of institution but rather expressed a general feeling that something ought to be done for the farmer and the mechanic, and that farming ought to be made more scientific. The Yale conversation included the interesting comment that "he did not intend them to be *agricultural* schools. The title of the bill was not his, and was not a very happy one. A clerk was responsible for the title."[9]

By the 1870's and 1880's, Morrill was talking not about colleges for agriculture and mechanical arts but about "national colleges for the advancement of general science and industrial education." When farm societies demanded that the land-grant colleges stress experimental farms and practical

[8] 14 *Stat.* 85 (1866).

[9] "Manuscript of a statement by Hon. Justin Morrill on the intent of the Land-Grant Act, 1862," quoted in True, *Agricultural Education*, 107–108. The title of the bill was "An Act Donating Public Lands to the Several States and Territories which may Provide Colleges for the Benefit of Agriculture and the Mechanic Arts."

agricultural courses, Morrill defended efforts to bring liberal culture to the industrial classes.[10] He said in 1888:

> The land-grant colleges were founded on the idea that a higher and broader education should be placed in every State within reach of those whose destiny assigns them to, or who may have the courage to choose industrial vocations where the wealth of nations is produced. . . . It would be a mistake to suppose it was intended that every student should become either a farmer or a mechanic when the design comprehended not only instruction for those who may hold a plow or follow a trade, but such instruction as any person might need . . . and without the exclusion of those who might prefer to adhere to the classics.[11]

Morrill's concern with equalizing educational opportunity among all states and for the less-privileged classes had its counterpart in the movement to create a federal department of education. The establishment of such an agency had long been a subject of debate. The matter came to a head in December 1865 when Congressman Ignatius Donnelly of Minnesota introduced a motion calling for "a national Bureau of Education, whose duty it shall be to enforce education, without regard to race or color, upon the population of all such states as shall fall below a standard to be established by Congress. . . ."[12] Strong opposition developed, but the bill finally passed both houses. It was strongly favored by the Republicans and was a substantially less extreme measure than that proposing the organization of a national system of education which came up in the same session of Congress.

As established March 2, 1867, the Department of Education had principally fact-finding power. Section 1 of the enabling act provided "that there shall be established a Department of Education for the purpose of collecting such

---

[10] Kandel, *Vocational Education*, 83–84.

[11] Honorable Justin Morrill, *Address* (1887), reprinted under the title *I Would Have Higher Education more widely Disseminated*, Amherst, Mass. (1961), 4.

[12] *Congressional Globe*, 39 Cong., 1 sess., 60.

statistics and facts as shall show the condition and progress of education in the several states and territories, and of diffusing such information." Hostility to the legislation survived its passage, and within one year the department was reduced to the Bureau of Education under the secretary of the interior. Even under these adverse conditions, the measure made an impact on Congress, for by 1869 both houses had established standing committees on education and labor to receive and review all educational proposals.

Amendments to the Morrill-Wade Act also involved the endowment funds provided by the act to be used to support the function of teaching or residential instruction in the land-grant colleges. It soon became clear that the grants would not provide adequate income for this purpose. Time limits for acceptance of the terms and establishing the institutions meant that states threw much of the land and scrip on the market at once. The flooding of the land market further depressed prices, which had already fallen way below the $1.25 per acre of federal evaluation. The Homestead Act and the railroad grants further provided competition, the former especially as it made land available to the settler without charge. The 1862 act had further required the states to sell their scrip to a third party rather than use it themselves to acquire title to land. Considering the depressed market and the competition, this requirement meant that speculators quickly came to dominate the resulting buyers' market.

As a consequence, the states received only a fraction of the endowment which Morrill and his colleagues had intended the act to provide. For example, Rhode Island assigned its 120,-000 acres of scrip to Brown University which, in turn, sold it to a private speculator for 42 cents an acre. New Hampshire sold its scrip for 53 cents an acre, and New Jersey for 55 cents an acre.[13]

In New York the story was substantially different, for Ezra Cornell purchased almost all of the 989,920 acres of scrip

[13] Benjamin Horace Hibbard, *A History of the Public Land Policies* (New York, 1939), 335–37.

assigned to the state at the market price of 60 cents an acre. Mr. Cornell then located 499,126 acres of this scrip in Wisconsin which, when sold, brought a net average price of $8.86 an acre. With other profits from the land, this money provided an endowment of over $5 million for Cornell University.[14]

The original legislation had thus failed to generate sufficient funds to finance the new educational program adequately. The state governments provided only marginal support and demands for the introduction of student tuition ran counter to Morrill's desire for free higher education. Not surprisingly, therefore, he turned again to the federal government in his efforts to secure additional endowment for the land-grant institutions.

Now a senator, Morrill began his long fight for further federal aid on February 23, 1872, when he introduced his bill S. 693:

> A bill to provide for the further endowment and support of
> colleges for the benefit of agriculture and mechanic arts,
> and the liberal and practical education of the industrial
> classes in the several pursuits and professions in life as estab-
> blished under an act of Congress approved July 2, 1862;
> by appropriating to each State in which such college may
> hereafter be established, one million acres of public lands, on
> such conditions as to use, application, and management of
> the sale and proceeds of such lands as are prescribed. . . .[15]

On March 11, Morrill reported this bill from the Committee on Education and Labor in substantially amended form. His amendments reduced the grant to the proceeds from the sale of 500,000 acres for each state and territory. The United States government was to hold the donated land until sold and then invest the proceeds in government 5 percent bonds to be held by the treasurer of the United States for the benefit of each land-grant institution. The government in this way could keep a lien on the endowment fund "to compel substantial and satis-

[14] Paul Wallace Gates, *The Wisconsin Pine Lands of Cornell University* (Ithaca, N. Y., 1943), 57, 242–43.
[15] *Congressional Globe*, 42 Cong., 2 sess., 275.

factory compliance with the conditions and limitations" of the grants. In his message accompanying the veto of Morrill's first bill in 1859, President Buchanan had objected that the government had no power to follow the funds into the state fiscal system to insure their proper use. Objection had also been made to the distribution by population under the 1862 act on the ground that the cost of starting a college was the same whether the states were large or small. The new provision that each state should receive an equal grant, along with the fiscal amendment, satisfied both of these objections.

The expressed opposition to this new bill reflected a change in the congressional climate of opinion. Though Senator William T. Hamilton of Maryland spoke of it as representing the "utter subversion of our republican form of government," the old constitutional argument had lost much of its force. Opposition rested mainly on much more pragmatic grounds. Senator John Sherman of Ohio served as the spokesman for this opposition and, in a speech on January 13, 1873, presented his major arguments. First, the government could not afford the loss of income that would result from the greatly reduced market price for public lands which would come on the market all at once. Second, if the land or money was to be distributed at all, it should be "in the same way that we are bound to levy taxes, namely, according to population." Third, Sherman insisted that the whole basis of the bill was wrong because, as he said, "the attempt to scatter these agricultural colleges into commercial States, into mining States, into banking States, into all kinds of States . . . seems utterly idle."[16] He argued that the bill represented the entering wedge of the national system of education then being debated. Finally, unwilling to gamble on a simple defeat of the bill by the regular voting process, Sherman moved to amend the measure, striking out all but the enacting clause and substituting aid for common schools.

Sherman's action with regard to common schools illustrated a problem of relationship which plagued Morrill for twenty

[16] Ibid., 3 sess., 525.

years in his efforts to obtain further aid for the land-grant colleges. The policy of land grants to the new states had combined federal aid to secondary and collegiate levels in the same measures. As indicated in the chapter on old states versus new, a new pattern emerged in the 1850's which separated proposals for schools from those supporting higher education. In 1870, Congressman George F. Hoar of Massachusetts introduced his famous bill to provide for a national system of common-school education maintained by federal authority. Morrill's bill passed the Senate but was blocked in the House. The Hoar bill and the subsequent Perce bill, also for support of secondary education, passed the House but not the Senate. Therefore, Morrill came increasingly to think it expedient to combine his efforts on behalf of the land-grant colleges with some kind of federal support for the common schools in the hope that the measure would pass both houses.

The two groups joined forces to push Morrill's next bill, S. 167, introduced on December 15, 1873. Under this measure receipts from the sale of public lands were to provide for the further endowment and support of the land-grant colleges "and to establish an educational fund, and apply the proceeds of a portion of the public lands to the support of public education. . . ."[17]

Unsuccessful with this bill, Morrill tried an identical bill in the next session of the same Congress, but with no better results. He then tried a change in tactics for his next effort. His new bill, S. 334, introduced on January 25, 1876, reversed the ordering of the two elements of his former bill so that the educational fund and support for common schools came first in the title of the bill. Moreover, instead of colleges for agriculture and the mechanical arts, Morrill now referred to the land-grant institutions as "national colleges for the advancement of general scientific and industrial education."

In urging passage of his bill, Morrill revived the memory of the famous clause in the Northwest Ordinance of 1787 that "religion, morality, and knowledge being necessary to good

[17] Ibid., 43 Cong., 1 sess., 188.

government and the happiness of mankind, schools and the means of education shall forever be encouraged." He insisted that this clause imposed a "national duty" not only on the states but on the federal government as well.[18] It will be recalled that even without any force in law, these well-known words had great effect as moral persuasion.

The Committee on Education and Labor, in reporting Morrill's bill, offered an amendment that would have substantially altered its nature. As amended, the fund for the first ten years would go to the states pro rata on the basis of the illiterate population over the age of ten. A portion of this money would go to the land-grant colleges, up to $30,000 per institution per year, with all the excess beyond that total going to help provide for free common-school education in the states and territories.[19] Clearly directed to the needs of the southern Negro, the amendment failed to stir sufficient congressional enthusiasm and died with the bill on the table in the Senate. Revival of interest at this time in the national university idea also helped kill both bill and amendment.

After several more attempts to get measures through both houses, Morrill added the debt payments of certain land-grant railroads to the money he would have the federal government dedicate to the support of education. On May 1, 1888, he introduced S. 2840, described as follows: "A bill to establish an educational fund and apply a portion of the proceeds of the public lands and receipts from certain land-grant railroad companies to public education, and to provide for a more complete endowment and support of colleges for the advancement of scientific and industrial education."[20]

This bill proved no more successful than any of the others, yet Morrill tried again an eleventh time in the third session of the Fifty-first Congress. Senator Henry W. Blair of New Hampshire, chairman of the Senate Committee on Education and Labor which received Morrill's new bill, S. 3256, was one

---

[18] *Congressional Record*, 44 Cong., 1 sess., 2761.
[19] Ibid., 2767.
[20] Ibid., 50 Cong., 1 sess., 3549.

of the strongest proponents of federal aid to common schools and the author of the Blair bill for federal support of common schools introduced on five separate occasions in the 1880's. Realizing that in their combined form neither federal aid to schools nor federal aid to land-grant colleges would probably pass both houses, Blair recommended that Morrill introduce a substitute bill eliminating any reference to public education or common schools.

Morrill accepted the advice and introduced a substitute measure, S. 3714, on April 30, 1890. He succeeded in this twelfth effort, for four months later the bill became what is known as the Second Morrill Act of 1890.[21]

The bill, S. 3714, received the full endorsement of the committee whose favorable report, S. 1028, alluded to the practical effects obtained in Europe by government support of agricultural education: wheat production tripled, acres under production doubled, crops per acre doubled, and the variety of crops greatly increased.

The report also spoke to the matter of the receipts from the land-grant railroads which had remained a part of Morrill's bill. The committee estimated the government debt of the railroads at $113,775,504. Morrill theorized that the debt would surely be paid and that over the years the payments could be dedicated to the support of the land-grant colleges. The committee thought, however, that if the support were appropriate, the money could be better taken directly from the treasury, thus avoiding roundabout and complicated financing.

Senator Preston B. Plumb of Kansas voiced the more general feeling in the Senate against inclusion of the railroad receipts. He objected to the permanent commitment of any public funds. His principal argument reflected his support of the Union Pacific Railroad, for whose interests he served as a congressional lobbyist. He asserted, moreover, that the Union Pacific was already negotiating a settlement with the United States government, and he wanted Congress to be under no

[21] 26 *Stat.* 417 (1890).

constraint in its relations with the company or with other rail-roads that would not permit Congress "to deal with them on the highest basis of public policy."

Congressional pressure forced the amendment of the bill, deleting the reference to the railroad debt. The financing provision of the bill then read as follows: "That there shall be, and hereby is, appropriated, out of any money in the Treasury not otherwise appropriated, arising from the sale of public lands, to be paid as hereinafter appropriated. . . ." The grants were to each state and territory "for the more complete endowment and support of colleges for the benefit of agriculture and mechanic arts."[22] Each grant amounted to $15,000 for the first year, increasing $1,000 annually for ten years and leveling off at $25,000.

Much argument developed over the subject areas to be included in the support provisions; this was particularly true in the House, where Congressman Louis E. McComas of Maryland had charge of the bill. The Farmers Alliance and the Patrons of Husbandry urged passage of an amendment requiring each state to replace money applied to instruction in any fields other than agriculture and mechanical arts. McComas, on the other hand, urged continued support of "the other scientific and classical studies" included in the 1862 act.[23] The House finally achieved a compromise between these two views by amending the bill to provide support as follows: "to be applied only to instruction in agriculture, the mechanic arts, the English language and the various branches of mathematical, physical, natural, and economic science with special reference to their applications in the industries of life, and to the facilities for such instruction." Although this language was

[22] While Morrill reverted to the language of the 1862 bill in describing the land-grant institutions, the Senate debate on the 1890 bill is listed in the index of the *Congressional Record* under "scientific and industrial education," not under "agriculture and mechanic arts."

[23] Following the pattern of the Morrill-Wade nomenclature for the first Morrill Act, it would be appropriate to designate the second Morrill Act as the Morrill-McComas Act because of McComas's significant part not only in its passage but also in its terms.

broader than that desired by farm interests, it still represented a considerable narrowing of scope as compared with the terms of the Morrill-Wade Act.

The House report on the bill, H. R. 2697, recognized that the state governments had come increasingly to the aid of the land-grant institutions in providing buildings and general budgets, and therefore good faith to the states required Congress to increase its provision of funds for instruction. The bill thus prohibited the use of any portion of the federal money for "the purchase, erection, preservation, or repair of any building or buildings."

The bill also contained provision for substantially increased federal supervision over the application of the funds. The measure required college presidents to submit "full and detailed annual reports" to both the secretary of the interior and the secretary of the treasury "regarding the condition and progress of each college." It further provided that these reports include an accounting of receipts and expenditures, library, faculty, students, and all "such other industrial and economic statistics as may be regarded as useful." Copies went free of cost to every other college under the franking privilege extended by Congress to the colleges endowed under the 1862 and 1890 acts. The secretary of the interior was authorized under the 1890 act to deny payments to any state which did not meet the conditions of the act and to report annually to Congress on the money disbursed or withheld. In this way, for the first time in federal grant procedure, the government established effective control over the use made of the granted funds.

In many ways the most striking feature of the Morrill-McComas Act was the guarantee that Negroes would benefit from its provisions. The Morrill-Wade Act passed before the Emancipation Proclamation and, specifically excluding the Confederate states, made no mention of the Negro. The Freedmen's Bureau, under Commissioner O. O. Howard, exhibited the first federal concern for the education of Negroes, but it was mainly at the common-school level, and in such a manner as to provide "the exercise of control without the burden of support."[24] However, in 1867, Congress incorporated Howard University in Washington, named for the commissioner and designed, with federal assistance, to serve the higher education needs of Negroes in the District.

By 1890 the southern states had accepted the terms of the Land-Grant College Act, and in many of these states separate and usually inferior institutions had been established for Negroes. Section 1 of the 1890 act provided that no money would be paid to a state or territory "where a distinction of race or color is made in the admission of students." Separate facilities, however, between which the funds were "equitably divided" would satisfy this provision. The act also allowed a state-supported college for Negroes not previously designated as a land-grant institution under the 1862 act now to be so designated, with the federal grant to the state being split between the two institutions on "a just and equitable" (but not necessarily equal) basis.

On the basis of population, the Negro has not received a proportionate share of these federal grants. In 1930, 23 percent of the population of the seventeen southern states was Negro. Yet as late as 1936, Negro colleges received only 6 percent of the federal funds apportioned to these states for support of land-grant colleges.[25] The funds appropriated under the 1890 act have, however, provided a significant portion of the money spent on Negro education in the South through the 1930's. Without these Negro land-grant institutions with their federal support, Negro education would have been immeasurably worse.

The federal government provided additional aid to the land-grant colleges as a result of an amendment to the 1907 Appropriations Act for the Department of Agriculture, introduced by Senator Knute Nelson of Minnesota. The Nelson Amendment granted an additional amount of $25,000 to each

[24] Gordon Canfield Lee, *The Struggle for Federal Aid, First Phase* (New York, 1949), 20.
[25] Edward Danforth Eddy, Jr., *Colleges for our Land and Time: The Land-Grant Idea in American Education* (New York, 1956), 263.

state and territory for the further endowment of these institutions to be paid in the manner prescribed by the 1890 act. The grants started at $5,000 a year for four years, with increases annually and leveling off at $25,000. The Nelson Amendment also provided the first grant for the support of teachers in allowing the right to use "a portion of this money for providing courses for the special preparation of instructors for teaching the elements of agriculture and the mechanic arts."[26]

The 1860 and 1890 acts and the Nelson Amendment, in providing basic federal support and the public recognition of the land-grant colleges and universities, stimulated the states to increase their aid to these institutions. In 1910 the federal aid to land-grant colleges amounted to one-third of their income. By 1932 this figure had dropped to 10 percent. But the government continued its aid in response to congressional pressure. The Bankhead-Jones Act of 1935, as amended in 1952 and 1960, provided the most recent examples of this aid.[27] Section 22 of this act granted $150,000 annually, plus variable amounts based on population, to each state and to Puerto Rico. The significant differences between this act and the Morrill and Nelson provisions are that the latter are permanent grants and in a sense automatic, whereas Congress must act on the Bankhead-Jones grants each year. In some years it has not appropriated the full amount authorized. The Morrill and Nelson grants also provided support principally for instruction in the land-grant institutions whereas the Bankhead-Jones provisions are related not only to instruction, but also to research, experiment stations, and extension, as discussed in the following chapter.

In 1893, Frederick Jackson Turner presented his famous thesis on the passing of the American frontier. By this time it was apparent that the importance of land as the major federal resource had also diminished. The 1862 Land-Grant College

---

[26] 34 *Stat.* 1282 (1907).
[27] 49 *Stat.* 436 (1935).

Act granted land, or scrip representing land, for support of education. The 1890 act moved one step away from the limitations of public-land-oriented federal grants by donating a portion of the receipts of the sale of land. In 1900, in a section of an Act Providing for Free Homesteads on the Public Lands, Congress stipulated "that in the event that the proceeds of the annual sale of public lands shall not be sufficient to meet the payments heretofore provided for agricultural colleges and experiment stations by Act of Congress, approved August thirtieth, eighteen hundred and ninety . . . such deficiency shall be paid by the United States . . . ."[28]

The progression from the 1862 to the 1890 Land-Grant College Act reveals several other important developments. The first act granted land to the states which they could dispose of in any way they desired. The second, reflecting the changes in the 1889 and subsequent grants to new states, discussed in the fourth chapter, made grants to the states with very specific requirements as to investment, yield, and preservation of principal. The first act also made a one-time grant, while the donations in the second act were based on annual appropriations.

In some respects, the relationship between these two acts resembled that between the 1787 Northwest Ordinance and the Ohio contracts.[29] The Northwest Ordinance is remembered for its language and the concept it espoused, while the Ohio contracts actually accomplished a great deal more of real significance. Likewise, the Morrill-Wade Act receives the place of public prominence, while the Morrill-McComas Act is relatively unknown. Yet, the second act, among other things, more than doubled the federal contribution to the land-grant colleges. The first is estimated to have produced $8.5 million by 1887, which, invested at 7 percent would have realized $600,-000 annually.[30] In the first year the second act provided $570,-000 and by 1900 over $1 million annually.

---

[28] 31 *Stat.* 179 (1900).
[29] Richard G. Axt, *The Federal Government and Financing Higher Education* (New York, 1952), 57.
[30] Blackmar, *Federal and State Aid*, 339–40.

Of importance in the history of federal legislation, the second act also produced patterns of control which influenced future grants. Under its terms the government specified what subjects would be supported with federal funds. The requirement of extensive annual reports found its origin here as well. The second act also contained the first withholding provision authorizing the government to assess penalties for noncompliance.[31] The pattern of diversity of responsibility in federal aid programs, which today finds government aid stemming from literally dozens of federal agencies, had a good start under the Morrill-McComas Act where the secretaries of agriculture, the interior, and the treasury were all involved in some manner.

In all these ways the Morrill-McComas Act resembles more a twentieth- than a nineteenth-century piece of federal legislation, and it serves well to illustrate changes in attitudes and governmental practices between these two centuries.

[31] V. O. Key, Jr., *The Administration of Federal Grants to States* (Chicago, 1937), 161.

9. FUNDS FOR EXPERIMENTATION

AND EXTENSION

·

In the years following the Civil War, the proposals for federal aid to education developed, spanning the entire educational spectrum and providing the basis of most of the important twentieth-century federal aid to education programs. The Blair and companion bills represented an effort to obtain aid for the common schools. Aid for vocational education at the secondary level provided the thrust of many schemes after the turn of the century. Some legislation initiated by Justin S. Morrill helped to establish, endow, and provide for general instruction in the land-grant colleges and universities. In the chronology of federal assistance to higher education the next major concern was to obtain federal support for research and experimentation in these land-grant institutions, and to extend beyond the classroom the benefits of the new knowledge thus derived.

Science and its application to the traditional fields of learning provided the major educational theme of the new land-grant institutions. Engineering and mechanical arts had become increasingly important educational programs since establishment of West Point in 1802. Students in industrial and mechanical studies far outnumbered those in agriculture by 1870, and the demand for trained engineers with competitive salaries increased faster than did that for agricultural scientists.[1]

It became quickly apparent to those teaching agriculture that the field could not yet be considered a science either in

[1] Kandel, *Vocational Education*, 102.

fact or in theory. After the farm student had exhausted the few standard works on scientific farming, there was nothing further available. The field required new knowledge both to establish the scientific basis of the study of agriculture and to answer the growing number of questions of farmers and farm societies. Yet this knowledge could only be supplied by research and experimentation. With no agreed-upon curriculum, no accepted methods of teaching, and no texts, teachers had to resort to experimental work.

Once again, Europe provided an example in the agricultural experiment stations scattered all over the Continent which directly applied science to farming. As early as 1871 the main theme at conventions of land-grant institutions was the need in the United States for such experiment stations associated with the land-grant colleges. Connecticut organized the first American experiment station in 1875, and within ten years fourteen other states had followed Connecticut's lead.[2]

The work of these stations solved a major problem for the land-grant colleges by providing a scientific basis for the new curriculum. But the second major problem of financing remained. By 1872 agricultural societies and the representatives of land-grant institutions had turned to the federal government for assistance in establishing and running these experiment stations.

The matter came to the floor of Congress in 1882 when Professor Seaman A. Knapp of the Iowa Agricultural College chaired a committee to draft a statement for the House Committee on Agriculture. From the statement came a bill "to establish national experiment stations in connection with the agricultural colleges of the various States." Congressman C. C. Carpenter of Iowa introduced the bill, H. R. 6110, in the House on May 8, 1882, where it unfortunately died in the Committee on Agriculture.[3]

[2] F. B. Mumford, *The Land-Grant College Movement* (Columbia, Mo., 1940), 87–89.
[3] *Congressional Record*, 47 Cong., 1 sess., 3704.

A convention of representatives of land-grant institutions then met in Washington in 1883 to endorse a proposal to establish experiment stations in connection with their institutions. At the urging of this body, on December 10, 1883, Congressman A. J. Holmes of Iowa introduced a modified form of the Carpenter bill seeking assistance from the federal Treasury for this purpose.[4]

As submitted, the Holmes Bill (H. R. 447) did not have the full endorsement of the land-grant institutions because it made the experiment stations virtually branches of the Department of Agriculture and put them to a considerable extent under the control of the commissioner.[5] The House Committee on Agriculture, headed by William Cullen of Illinois, nevertheless reported the bill favorably although with numerous amendments. As amended, the bill retained its objective "to aid the Department of Agriculture in the acquiring and diffusing of agricultural knowledge." The stations now, however, became distinct departments of the land-grant institutions, under the control of their respective boards of trustees or regents, and making their reports to their respective state governors, not to the commissioner of agriculture.

Congress was not yet ready to pass such an aid bill, and the representatives of the land-grant institutions met again in Washington to urge action. At that meeting, in 1885, Professor Knapp expressed the general feeling when he commented:

> I think all thoughtful men have long since agreed upon two questions: First, the necessity of accurate experimentation, in charge of trained men, to determine the important agricultural problems that now confront the people of this great producing country; and, secondly, that it is impossible that the investigation should be carried on by private means.[6]

The convention then passed the following resolution:

[4] Ibid., 48 Cong., 1 sess., 73.
[5] True, *Agricultural Education*, 205.
[6] Quoted in Eddy, *Colleges for our Land and Time*, 96.

That the condition and progress of American agriculture require national aid for investigation and experimentation in the several States and Territories; and that therefore this convention approves the principle and general provisions of what is known as the Cullen Bill of the last Congress, and urges upon the next Congress the passage of this or a similar act.[7]

In addition, thirty-five states submitted petitions to the Forty-ninth Congress urging the establishment of agricultural experiment stations connected with the land-grant colleges and universities.[8] As a result of this, and of the general feeling that the benefits of investigation would accrue both to the farmer and to the entire population, three bills were introduced in the Senate and nine in the House calling for federal aid for these stations.

The bill that eventually passed both houses and became law became known as the Hatch Act, named for Congressman William H. Hatch of Missouri, chairman of the House Committee on Agriculture. In fact, the bill which he pushed through the House was not his own bill, though he introduced one similar to it, but was Senate bill S. 372, introduced by Senator J. Z. George of Mississippi on December 10, 1885.[9] The two bills even had the same title—"A bill to establish agricultural experiment stations in connection with the colleges established in the several States under the provisions of an act approved July 2, 1862, and of act supplementary thereto." Following the pattern of the Morrill-Wade and Morrill-McComas acts, perhaps the measure should more properly have been called the Hatch-George Act.

The Senate Committee on Agriculture and Forestry considered the George bill and reported it back favorably but with considerable amendments on April 26, 1886. After much debate the bill finally passed the Senate on January 27, 1887,

---

[7] A. C. True and V. A. Clark, *The Agricultural Experiment Stations in the United States* (Washington, D. C., 1900), 35–36.

[8] *Congressional Record*, 49 Cong., 2 sess., index p. 2.

[9] Ibid., 29 Cong., 1 sess., 154.

going thence to the House. The Hatch bill, H. R. 2933, drafted with the help of Norman J. Colman, commissioner of agriculture, was already under consideration, having been submitted to the House on January 7, 1886.

The George bill went to the Committee on Agriculture, of which Hatch was chairman, and Hatch reported it back favorably for his committee on March 3, with the following comment:

> the Committee deem it unnecessary to enlarge upon the importance of the end to be attained. No principle is better established among civilized nations than that the prosperity of agriculture involves that of every other interest. No conviction is stronger or more universal among our own people than that it is the duty of the Government, by every legitimate means in its power, to aid in preserving and developing the agricultural resources of the country, thereby promoting the welfare not only of those who make this branch of industry the business of their lives, but that of every other class of citizen.[10]

Hatch went on to point out that he sought an appropriation of only $15,000 per station, the basic amount set out in the Carpenter, Holmes, and Cullen bills, or $570,000 for all states. This, he claimed, was a very small sum to request for the special improvement of an industry which required the labor of 7.5 million men and gave direct support to one-half the population; an industry which had $10 billion invested in its lands, $400 million in its implements and machinery, and $1.5 million in its livestock; and an industry which produced $2.2 billion worth of products annually.

Since the George bill had already passed the Senate, Hatch agreed to accept it in the House in substitution for his own bill. He was successful in pushing the George bill through the House, and President Cleveland signed it on March 2, 1887.[11] The language of the bill declared the purpose of this federal support of agricultural research:

[10] *House Report 848*, 49 Cong., 1 sess., 2.
[11] 24 *Stat.* 440 (1887).

that in order to aid in acquiring and diffusing among the
people of the United States useful and practical information
on subjects connected with agriculture, and to promote
scientific investigation and experiment respecting the principles and applications of agricultural science, there shall be
established, under direction of the college or colleges or
agricultural department of colleges in each State or Territory established, or which may hereafter be established, in
accordance with the provisions of an act . . . [the Morrill
Act of 1862 and its supplements] a department to be known
and designated as an "agricultural experiment station."

The appropriations section of the act stipulated that aid was
given specifically to assist in "paying the necessary expenses
of conducting investigations and experiments and printing and
distributing the results." For this purpose, Congress appropriated the sum of $15,000 per year for each station, to be
paid "to the treasurer or other officer duly appointed by the
governing boards of said colleges to receive the same."

This language signified important modifications in the previous manner of granting federal aid to education. Up to 1887
grants to the states had been in the form of land or lump sums
of money. The Hatch Act now introduced the system of annual
payments, or subventions, which has characterized federal
aid ever since. The modern significance of this feature lies in
the degree of federal control which it has been possible to
exercise through successive annual payments.[12]

The provision for direct payment to the institution and
not to the state or territory was also a substantial innovation,
and this too has characterized most twentieth-century federal
grants. An added new financial requirement directed that any
appropriated funds remaining unused at the end of the year
would be deducted from the next year's appropriation.

The act also stipulated that the money be appropriated
from treasury funds derived from the sale of public lands.
Since 1888, however, the annual appropriation for the experiment stations has been included as a line item in the

---

[12] Hill and Fisher, *Basic Facts*, 38.

regular budget of the Department of Agriculture.[13] This perfunctory inclusion provides another example of the decreasing importance of the public lands as a prime federal financial resource.

To insure the adequate supervision of expenditures, the act required each station to submit annually "a full and detailed report" of its operations, including a statement of receipts and expenditures. Copies of these reports went to the commissioner (now secretary) of agriculture, the secretary of the treasury, and to all other stations. To facilitate the satisfaction of the latter provision, Congress extended the franking privilege to the institutions. By insisting on these financial reports, Congress took a first major step towards the current system of federal audits of the spending of federal grants which now characterizes present programs of federal aid to education.

The act further required each station, in addition to its annual report, to publish bulletins and reports of progress at least every three months so there would be prompt distribution of information resulting from the experiments. These bulletins went to each newspaper in the state territory and to any interested individual requesting the same.

Reasonable uniformity of standards in the methods and results of the work of the stations was desirable and the act authorized the commissioner of agriculture to furnish forms for the tabulation of results of investigations and experiments. He was also authorized "to indicate, from time to time, such lines of inquiry as to him shall seem most important, and in general to furnish such advice and assistance as will best promote the purpose of this Act."

Congress then established the Office of Experiment Stations in 1888 to represent the commissioner of agriculture in his relations with the stations. In 1894, Congress inserted in the appropriations act the following provision: "The Secretary of Agriculture shall prescribe the form of the annual financial statement, shall ascertain whether expenditures under the ap-

---

[13] True, *Agricultural Education*, 209–10.

propriation hereby made are in accordance with the provisions of said Act, and shall report thereon to Congress."

The Hatch Act greatly stimulated the growth and development of the agricultural experiment stations and agricultural research. Between 1887 and 1900 the number of these stations increased markedly and their caliber improved.

For many reasons education in engineering and the other mechanical arts did not enjoy the same federal support as did that in agriculture, even though engineering attracted more students. There was no such well-defined group as the farmer to lobby for engineering. Private industry tended to dominate engineering research because new discoveries could readily be patented and turned to commercial advantage. Moreover, engineering curricula had already begun to be developed in the state universities by 1862, and competition between these and the land-grant institutions prevented the quick growth of engineering at the latter. Thus a bill to obtain federal funds for engineering experiment stations introduced in 1907 by Congressman William McKinley of Illinois never emerged from the House Committee on Agriculture, to which it had been referred.

Engineering experiment stations did develop, however, patterned after the successful agricultural stations. The University of Illinois in 1903 became the first land-grant institution to establish such a separate station.[14] But the real growth of federal interest in engineering research had to wait for its development until the pressures of World War I had their effect.

The work of these agricultural and engineering stations substantially changed the character of the land-grant colleges. For the first time research became an established college function, with faculty dividing their time between the classroom and the laboratory or the experiment station. But this did not happen without struggle, for to some educators even then research and teaching were in conflict. When the Morrill-

---

[14] Eddy, *Colleges for our Land and Time*, 128.

McComas Act of 1890 provided additional funds for instruction, this in some cases released Hatch Act funds for experiment work which had been supporting instruction up to that point, contrary to law.[15]

Concern over the nature of the research to be undertaken was also evident. At first the stations had been occupied with the solution of the immediate, practical problems confronting the farmer in his locality, state, or region. The factor of immediate and demonstrable economic utility played a large part in helping to secure the endorsement and support of local farm groups. The Hatch Act had prescribed specific kinds of practical or applied research, including the following:

> physiology of plants and animals; the diseases to which they are severally subject, with remedies for the same; the chemical composition of useful plants at their different states of growth; the comparative advantages of rotative cropping as pursued under the varying series of crops; the capacity of new plants or trees for acclimation; the analysis of soils and water; the chemical composition of manures, natural or artificial, with experiments designed to test the comparative effects on crops of different kinds; the adaptation and value of grasses and forage plants; the composition and digestibility of the different kinds of food for domestic animals; the scientific and economic questions involved in the production of butter and cheese . . . .

Yet the need for original research could not be overlooked. As prosperity replaced depression in agriculture after the turn of the century, station personnel became freer to concentrate on pure research. In this effort researchers secured the assistance of Congressman Henry Cullen Adams of Wisconsin, who had long been identified with the farming and dairy interests of his state and region and was to become a prime mover in the passage of the Pure Food and Drug Act of 1906. On December 4, 1905, Adams introduced H. R. 345, a bill "to provide for an increased annual appropriation for

[15] Ross, *Democracy's Colleges*, 141.

agricultural experiment stations, and regulating the expense thereof."[16]

The bill went to the House Committee on Agriculture, and Adams reported it back favorably on January 15, 1906. In his report he described with great enthusiasm the work of the forty-eight stations then in operation and indicated that the growth of the farm portion of the national economy, together with the larger demands made on these stations, more than justified an increase in their annual appropriations.

The Adams bill called for an initial additional appropriation of $5,000 for each station, with an addition of $2,000 a year for five years until a total increase of $15,000 was reached. This stipulation in effect doubled the annual appropriation under the Hatch Act to $30,000 a year.

Debate on the Adams bill was complicated by the insistence of Congressman Sereno Payne of New York, chairman of the House Ways and Means Committee, that it be coupled in debate with his bill "to provide for the consolidation and reorganization of customs collection districts and other purposes." Adams finally secured the passage of his bill by explaining that it was "simply a reenactment of the Hatch Act in every respect except the additional amount which is granted to the experiment stations." The bill then passed the House and went to the Senate. There the Committee on Agriculture and Forestry reported favorably, and passing the Senate, the bill received the signature of President Theodore Roosevelt on March 16, 1906.[17]

Adams was not altogether accurate in his comment about the relationship between his bill and the Hatch Act, for his bill incorporated many of the new legislative features introduced by the Morrill-McComas Act in 1890. These included the prescription on the replacement of lost or diminished funds and the federal control exercised through the provision for withholding certification of allotments, which power the Adams Act delegated to the secretary of agriculture. The

[16] *Congressional Record*, 59 Cong., 1 sess., 52.
[17] 34 *Stat.* 63 (1906).

Adams Act also incorporated the 1890 act provision making payment by the secretary of the treasury subject to the warrant of the secretary of agriculture.

The most significant difference between the Hatch and Adams acts, however, had to do with the nature of the research to be supported. Where the Hatch Act had stipulated support of specific practical applied research, the Adams Act considerably changed the authorized activity by providing that the appropriation be applied only to paying the necessary expenses of conducting original research.

Three subsequent acts have added considerably to the extent of federal support of these Hatch Act stations. The agricultural depression of the 1920's focused the need for research in national problems of marketing and distribution rather than on local or regional problems of production. As a consequence, the Purnell Act of 1925 authorized the expenditure of money for various kinds of economic and sociological investigation in addition to the more traditional agricultural research.[18] The purpose of the research was to assist in "the establishment and maintenance of a permanent and efficient agricultural industry . . . [and] the development and improvement of the rural home and rural life. . . ." Toward this objective the act authorized an increased initial annual appropriation of $20,000, with annual increases of $10,000 until the added amount totaled $60,-000. This increase, with the previously authorized $30,000, brought the level of support for each experiment station to $90,000 annually.

The depression of the 1930's further accelerated the trend from production research to broader considerations of the relation of the farm sector to the entire economy. Since the depression was clearly a national problem, cooperative research among stations was stressed in those sections of the Bankhead-Jones Act of 1935 which dealt with the experiment stations.[19] Several other new concepts appeared in this act. An annual added appropriation of $1 million was authorized, with annual

[18] 43 *Stat.* 970 (1925).
[19] 49 *Stat.* 436 (1935).

increases up to $5 million. But this amount did not go to the stations equally, as in previous legislation, but in proportion to rural population. Equality in the House of Representatives based on population became the standard, replacing equality as between states measured in the Senate. A new trend for federal appropriations illustrated the growing importance of government agencies in that 40 percent of the money appropriated went to the Department of Agriculture to be spent on departmental research. This left only 60 percent to be distributed to the stations, which they were also required to match.

The features of the matching requirement, cooperative research, distribution of funds on the basis of population, and division of funds between the stations and the department were all repeated in the Research and Marketing Act of 1946, which authorized added appropriations.[20]

In summary then, the Morrill-Wade Act and its supplements provided federal support for the establishment and endowment of the land-grant colleges. These funds were directed specifically to support of instruction. The Hatch Act and its supplements provided federal support for the research function within these institutions. But it soon became clear that however much the land-grant institutions might stress the teaching of agriculture and mechanic arts, the majority of students were not studying these subjects but were enrolled in the more traditional degree programs. For the year 1872 the House Committee on Education and Labor reported that only 130 out of 478 students had graduated in agriculture.[21] Later, in his 1890–1891 Report, the United States commissioner of education confirmed the view that "even the most cursory examination of colleges thus aided [by the Morrill legislation] will show that in the large majority of cases these branches [agriculture and mechanical arts] have not been made the 'leading objects' " as the Morrill legislation required. As late as 1915 the commissioner reported that only 23.1

[20] 60 *Stat.* 1082 (1946).
[21] *House Report 57*, 43 Cong., 2 sess., 36–37.

percent of the total instructional expenditure for the land-grant colleges went for instruction in agriculture.[22]

These figures help to illustrate two related problems. First, the majority of students in the agricultural colleges did not study farming even though they came from farm families. Second, the benefits of research and instruction in agriculture did not reach the farmer because he was not in college but on the farm. Farm groups such as the National Grange and the Farmers' Alliance espoused these views and claimed that the instruction in the new land-grant institutions was too theoretical, offering nothing to the average farmer. Particularly was this the case where Morrill funds had been used to graft agricultural courses onto the programs of already established classical colleges.

As a consequence, by the mid-1860's farm societies began to sponsor farmers' institutes which offered short practical courses in agriculture. Often these programs were assisted and in many cases run by the personnel of the land-grant institutions. By 1907 over one-half of the land-grant institutions had developed some kind of extension program designed to spread the benefits of the new findings in agricultural research beyond the classroom. These short courses provided the basis of the elaborate extension program developed in the twentieth century. Related to the land-grant colleges, these programs were justified by the democratic ideal of the Morrill legislation of extending education to the people. By 1912 there were 6,778 of these programs, enrolling almost 2,550,-000 farmers.[23]

From 1903 to 1914 the federal government was active in the extension field. Under the authority of the commerce clause of the Constitution, Congress provided funds for federal demonstration agents working first in the areas of the South and West stricken by the boll weevil. By 1914, Congress was spending over $400,000 a year on this program of informa-

[22] Kandel, *Vocational Education*, 102.
[23] Alfred C. True, *A History of Agricultural Extension Work in the United States, 1785–1923* (Washington, D. C., 1928), 32.

tion and demonstration of new methods of pest control and fertilization.

Then on May 8, 1914, the president signed the Smith-Lever Act, a compromise of sixteen bills then pending before Congress.[24] Drafted by Congressman Ashbury Lever of South Carolina and Senator Hoke Smith of Georgia, the Smith-Lever bill was introduced in the House and Senate on June 12, 1911, and July 16, 1912, respectively. The purpose of the act was to finance a program of cooperation between the land-grant colleges and the Department of Agriculture "in order to aid in diffusing among the people of the United States useful and practical information on subjects relating to agriculture and home economics, and to encourage the application of the same" by persons not attending college.

In support of this objective the act provided an annual appropriation of $10,000 for each state which accepted the provision of the act by legislative assent. Congress authorized an additional total of $600,000, increased by $500,000 a year for seven years, which would be distributed to the states "in the proportion which the rural population of each State bears to the total rural population of all the States."

The provisions to which the states had to assent were the most exacting of any federal grant thus far passed by Congress. A director attached to the land-grant institution carried out the extension program. His appointment, and that of any other personnel supported by the federal funds, required approval of the secretary of agriculture. Following the precedent established in the 1911 Maritime Academies Aid Act, annual federal funds could not be paid until they had been matched by an equal amount "appropriated for that year by the legislature of such State, or provided by State, county, college local authority, or individual contributions from within the State." Finally, and most severely, the federal funds would be granted only when the extension program proposed by the college or state had received the prior approval of the Federal Extension Division of the Department of Agriculture. Funds, even if

[24] 38 *Stat.* 372 (1914).

already appropriated, could be withheld by the secretary to insure conformity with the act.

Perhaps owing to the direct contact with the local farmer, increased federal funds for extension were easily obtained. The Clarke-McNary Act of 1924, the Clapper-Ketchem Act of 1928, the Bankhead-Jones Act of 1935, and the Bankhead-Flannagan Act of 1946 all provided added annual appropriations for extension. By 1951, the land-grant college annual appropriation for instruction reached $5 million; for experiment stations, $12 million; and for extension, $32 million.[25] In 1953 the Hope-Aiken Act consolidated all the federal extension legislation, removing the confusion between matching and nonmatching, rural-population-based and farmer-population-based, and permanent and annual grants. It allowed Congress to allocate the annual amount for extension on the basis of an open-ended appropriation.

As discontent by the farmer with the existing pattern of educational opportunity led to the federally supported extension program, so discontent among industrial workers led to a federally supported program of vocational education. This was not a college-level or even a college-associated program as it emerged in the Smith-Hughes Act of 1917, but it represented the logical extension of the land-grant college program.[26] As sponsored by Senator Hoke Smith, it resembled the Smith-Lever Act and other land-grant college legislation in being directed to mass education, to publicly supported education, and to practical, vocational education—all carried on under growing federal supervision. Each of these characteristics came increasingly to represent the early twentieth-century movement in federal aid to education away from general, arms-length support of higher education as a desirable social objective, and toward support of specific kinds of practical education designed to satisfy the needs of discrete groups within the society.

[25] Commission on Intergovernmental Relations, "A Description of Twenty-five Federal Grant-in-Aid Programs" (Washington, D. C., June, 1955), 30.
[26] 39 *Stat.* 929 (1917).

Looking back over the history of the early period of federal activity affecting the financing of higher education, we can identify five categories of development: the objectives of the legislation enacted, the kinds of educational programs assisted or established, the recipients or beneficiaries of federal grants, the conditions of the grants, and the resources granted. It is important now to ask what we can learn from a review of this history that provides some insight useful to the discussion of problems of federal aid in the mid-twentieth century.

It seems clear from the evidence that during the period examined the federal government approached aid to education as a means rather than as an end in itself. The educational benefit derived from an increase in individual growth and competence appears to have been sought only as a by-product. Some more immediate objectives of congressional legislation which provided aid to education have been to undergird the existing social structure in the colonial period, to facilitate the sale of the public land in the Confederation period, to aid in the development of new public-land states throughout the nineteenth century, to cement the internal unity of the Republican party and balance the interests of landless and landed states in the 1860's, and to answer the demands of increasingly politically powerful special-interest groups, such as the farmer, at the turn of the century. The post–World War II G. I. bill and the 1965 National Defense Education Act provide the twentieth-century extension of this thrust.

Still, it is difficult to determine what caused the passage of any of the pieces of legislation discussed. Educational theories, group demands for wider educational opportunity, economic and political considerations of public lands, political expediency, tariff, and tax policy all played their part then as they do in the enactment of any twentieth-century legislation. It is interesting to note, however, as for example in the case of the Ohio Company Contract of 1787 and the Morrill legislation of 1862, that educational grants were deemed the best means of accomplishing other objectives.

Whatever the specific objectives of any individual piece of

legislation, it is clear that the educational thrust of the legislation considered was to broaden educational opportunity, to help recognize and to secure the place of science in the educational curriculum, and to move from general support of higher education to support of specific educational programs. Legislation such as the Morrill-Wade Act of 1862 also initiated the process of equalization of opportunity so characteristic of twentieth-century federal educational legislation by taking land from the landed states and giving it to the landless for educational purposes.

The changes in the objectives of legislation discussed and the changes in combinations of political forces which secured passage of legislative acts, are in part evident in the changing character of the programs supported. While in the colonial period education largely reinforced class position, in the increasingly democratic nineteenth century, education became a major vehicle of social and economic mobility. From early concern with the establishment of a national university to train national leadership, Congress moved first to support widespread public higher education and then public vocational education below the college level.

As the nature of the federally aided programs narrowed during the latter half of the nineteenth century, so the recipients and beneficiaries of federal aid became increasingly specific. The Ohio Company Contract granted land "for the purposes of a university . . . to be applied to the intended objects by the Legislature of the State." Grants to the new states then designated public universities as the beneficiaries. In the Morrill legislation of 1862 only specific kinds of institutions received aid. Finally, in the Hatch Act of 1887, the institutions themselves became the initial recipients, bypassing the states as intermediaries. It was only a short step to the twentieth-century policy of making grants to individuals such as in the post–World War II G. I. Bill of Rights and National Defense Education acts.

Accompanying the above two changes of program and recipient, the conditions of the federal grants became increasingly exacting. From the earlier grants to the Ohio Company and the new states over which Congress exercised little or no control, the spectrum spread to the 1917 Smith-Hughes requirements of prior executive approval, annual financial reporting, and withholding provisions. During the same period, Congress also moved from the single land grant for endowment to the specific annual appropriation from general tax revenues for current expenses.

It can be said then that federal assistance to higher education in the nineteenth century moved from a single, broad-scale program of endowment grants to support education to a series of piecemeal efforts to aid education through a broad range of special-interest programs. Money from federal land grants represented the major portion of the first educational budgets of many of the new states. Land-grant colleges and experiment and extension programs were all financed primarily by federal money at their inception.

In the early twentieth century federal interest in higher education splintered into half a dozen programs in most of which the federal funds bore a minority position to state and local support. For example, federal contributions to operating receipts for all land-grant institutions fell from 34.2 percent in 1900 to 11.9 percent in 1920.[27] By 1920 also, federal spending on general higher education through the Office of Education amounted to only $306,629 as against $11,620,-000 spent on special programs, such as experiment and extension administered through other agencies.[28] In spite of the great increase in the dollar amounts involved, federal support of education in the nineteenth century became federal aid in the twentieth.

---

[27] U. S., Congress, House, *Annual Reports of the Department of the Interior: Report of the Commissioner of Education*, 56 Cong., 2 sess., 1900, *House Document 5 2*:2064–65; U. S., Department of the Interior, Office of Education, *Survey of Land-Grant Colleges and Universities* (Washington, D. C., 1930), 54–59.

[28] U. S., Department of the Interior, Bureau of Education, *Agricultural and Mechanical Colleges, Bulletin No. 8* (Washington, D. C., 1920), 32–34, 39, 41.

There is a curious irony about this changed relationship of the federal government to higher education. The loudest voices raised in contemporary discussions of the efficacy of federal aid are those denouncing the potentiality of federal control. The irony exists in the fact that in the early programs of federal land grants to new states when the government actually underwrote the common-school and state university programs, it did so with almost no controls attached. The principal argument in opposition then was not so much that Congress would improperly control local educational institutions, but rather that the federal government had no constitutional power to assist these institutions. Now that the federal contribution to education has decreased proportionately to the amount of state and local assistance, the constitutional argument seems less potent (particularly after the 1965 General Aid to Education Act), but the fear of federal control has increased.

It is also important to recall that what federal control now exists, as exercised through the requirements of financial reporting and program approval, arose as a result of the failure of state government adequately to conserve and to utilize the grants of land to new states or the land and scrip grants of the 1862 Morrill legislation. Yet the new state and Morrill grants cannot serve as examples of federal control of education. In fact, the reverse is more accurate. In the colonial period private colleges and universities gratefully received public financial assistance in a context which allowed them to retain their private status. Control and management remained private even though financing was semipublic. Although the nineteenth-century land-grant institutions were financed by federal grants, they were clearly under local control, either public or private. The 1950 report of the Hoover Commission Task Force on Public Welfare stated the case well:

> The land-grant colleges have been an outstanding example of federal promotion of state leadership and initiation. The very large local support as compared with the relatively small present federal assistance is witness to this fact. . . .

We have demonstrated through these programs that the federal government can promote specific causes in the fields of education whereby initiative and responsibility can be properly retained by the states.[29]

The study of the record of the nineteenth century then documents several facts which should not be ignored in current discussions of federal aid to education. The first is that federal assistance does not necessarily establish federal control. The second is that however desirable federal aid may be to educators or the public at large, Congress is more likely to pass, and the president to sign, legislation if federal aid is tied to, or combined with, other less historically controversial social objectives.

[29] Hollis P. Allen, *The Federal Government and Education* (New York, 1950), 219.

Appendix A

MAJOR EDUCATIONAL

ENACTMENTS

.

1785 Land Ordinance; first reservation of land for schools.
1787 Northwest Ordinance. Ohio Company of Associates contract; first reservation of land for higher education.
1802 Ohio Enabling Act; pattern of land grants established for new states.
1803 Ohio Enabling Act Amendment; Five Per Cent Grant established.
1830 First federal research contract with Franklin Institute.
1836 Deposit Act.
1841 Distribution–Pre-emption Act. Internal Improvement Grants of 500,000 acres for new states.
1850 Swamp and Overflow Land Grants for new states.
1862 Morrill Land-Grant College Act (Morrill-Wade Act).
1867 Department of Education established. Howard University established; supported with federal funds.
1887 Hatch Act; experiment stations, first annual grants for general support.
1889 Enabling Act for North and South Dakota, Montana, and Washington; pattern of grants for new states changed.
1890 Second Morrill Act (Morrill-McComas Act).
1906 Adams Act; added support for experiment stations.
1907 Nelson Amendment; added support for land-grant institutions.
1914 Smith-Lever Act; agricultural extension.
1917 Smith-Hughes Act; vocational education.

LAND GRANTS FOR HIGHER

EDUCATION

.

State	Land Grants for New States[a] (in acres)	Morrill and Supplementary Grants[b] (in acres)	Average Sale Price per Acre of Morrill Land[c]
Alabama	142,160	240,000*	$ 1.06
Arizona	696,080	150,000	(no data)
Arkansas	46,080	150,000*	0.88
Alaska	[d]	436,000	(no data)
California	46,080	150,000	4.93
Connecticut	—	180,000*	0.75
Delaware	—	90,000*	0.92
Florida	92,160	90,000*	1.71
Georgia	—	270,000*	0.90
Hawaii	[e]	[f]	—
Idaho	296,080	90,000	7.78
Illinois	46,080	480,000	1.35
Indiana	88,160[g]	390,000*	0.87
Iowa	46,080	240,000	3.37
Kansas	46,080	90,000	5.97
Kentucky	—	330,000*	0.44
Louisiana	46,080	210,000*	0.87
Maine	—	210,000*	0.56
Maryland	—	210,000*	0.55
Massachusetts	—	360,000*	0.61
Michigan	46,080	240,000	4.23
Minnesota	92,160	120,000	6.14
Mississippi	92,160[h]	210,000*	0.47
Missouri	46,080	330,000	1.32
Montana	246,080	140,000	4.90
Nebraska	46,080	90,000	6.86
Nevada	46,080	90,000	1.35
New Hampshire	—	150,000*	0.53

State	Land Grants for New States[a] (in acres)	Morrill and Supplementary Grants[b] (in acres)	Average Sale Price per Acre of Morrill Land[c]
New Jersey	—	210,000*	0.55
New Mexico	961,000	250,000	(no data)
New York	—	990,000*	0.70
North Carolina	—	270,000*	0.46
North Dakota	206,080	130,000	10.90
Ohio	69,120	630,000*	0.83
Oklahoma	650,000[i]	250,000	(no data)
Oregon	46,080	90,000	2.28
Pennsylvania	—	780,000*	0.66
Rhode Island	—	120,000*	0.42
South Carolina	—	180,000*	0.53
South Dakota	206,080	160,000	2.44
Tennessee	—	300,000*	1.33
Texas	—	180,000*	1.16
Utah	356,080	200,000	(no data)
Vermont	—	150,000*	0.90
Virginia	—	300,000*	1.15
Washington	246,080	90,000	3.91
West Virginia	—	150,000*	0.77
Wisconsin	92,160	240,000	1.27
Wyoming	46,080	90,000	0.61

* Designates those states receiving scrip.

[a] Based on U. S., General Land Office, School Lands, Information Bulletin No. 1 (Washington, D. C., 1939), 3–11.

[b] Based on U. S., Department of the Interior, Office of Education. *Agricultural and Mechanical Colleges. Bulletin No. 8* (Washington, D. C., 1920), 31.

[c] Based on Benjamin H. Hibbard, *A History of the Public Land Policies* (New York, 1939), 335–37.

[d] It is impossible to tell how much of the 102,550,000 acres granted to Alaska in 1958 was used for higher education.

[e] Hawaii received all title to U. S. lands within its boundaries upon admission, in lieu of a grant of land (see text, p. 51).

[f] Hawaii received a grant of $6 million in the Hawaii Omnibus Act of 1960, in lieu of a land grant (see text, p. 52).

[g] This includes the 19,040 acres granted to the state university in 1854 (see text, p. 50) and 23,040 acres granted to Vincennes University on Mar. 3, 1873 (see Hibbard, 342).

[h] This includes 23,040 acres granted to Jefferson College on Mar. 3, 1803 (see Hibbard, 342).

[i] This does not include the special fund (see text, p. 50).

BIBLIOGRAPHY

.

UNPUBLISHED MATERIALS

Clark, Duncan Ellsworth. "Nationalism in Education revealed in Congressional Action to 1862." Ph.D. diss., Stanford University, 1930.

Cowley, W. H. "A Short History of American Higher Education." Unpublished MS, Stanford University, 1961.

Germann, George B. "National Legislation Concerning Education: Its Influence and Effect in the Public Land States East of the Mississippi admitted prior to 1800." Ph.D. diss., Columbia University, 1899.

Harrison, Theta. "History of the Movement for a National University in the United States." Ph.D. diss., Stanford University, 1931.

Merrill, George Donald. "Land and Education—The Origin and History of Land Grants for the Support of Education." Ed.D. diss., University of Southern California, 1965.

Smith, Willard W. "The Relations between Colleges and Government in Colonial America." Ph.D. diss., Columbia University, 1950.

GOVERNMENT DOCUMENTS

Acts of the General Assembly of Connecticut with Other Permanent Documents Respecting Yale University. New Haven, 1901.

Addis, Wellford. "Federal and State Aid to Higher Education," *Report of the United States Commissioner of Education, 1896–7* (1898), 1137–64.

Bartlett, John Russell, ed. *Records of the Colony of Rhode Island and Providence Plantations, in New England.* 10 vols. Providence, 1856–1865.

Blauch, Lloyd E. *Federal Cooperation in Agricultural Education Work, Vocational Education, and Vocational Rehabilitation.* United States Department of the Interior, *Bulletin No. 15.* Washington, D. C., 1933.

Bouton, Nathaniel, ed. *Provincial papers. Documents and records relating to the province of New Hampshire from the earliest period of its settlement: 1623–[1776].* 7 vols. Nashua, N. H., 1867–1873.

Brunner, Henry S. *Land-Grant Colleges and Universities, 1862–1962.* United States Office of Education, *Bulletin No. 13.* Washington, D. C., 1962.

Commission on Intergovernmental Relations. "A Description of Twenty-five Federal Grant-in-Aid Programs." Washington, D. C., June, 1955.

Elliot, Jonathan, ed. *Debates on the Adoption of the Federal Constitution, in the Convention held in Philadelphia in 1787.* 5 vols. Washington, D. C., 1836–1845.

Ford, W. C., et al., eds. *Journals of the Continental Congress, 1774–1789.* 34 vols. Washington, D. C., 1904–1937.

Hill, David S., and Fisher, William A. *Basic Facts.* Pt. 2 of *Federal Relations to Education—Report of the National Advisory Committee on Education.* 2 vols. Washington, D. C., 1931.

Keesecker, Ward W. *Digest of Legislation Providing Federal Subsidies for Education.* United States Office of Education. Washington, D. C., September 1929.

Klein, Arthur J., ed. *Survey of Land-Grant Colleges and Universities.* United States Office of Education, *Bulletin No. 9.* 2 vols. Washington, D. C., 1930.

Lind, George, ed. *Statistics of Land-Grant Colleges and Universities—Year ending June 30, 1963.* United States Office of Education. Washington, D. C., 1965.

Miller, Helen A., and Shea, Andrew J. *Federal Assistance for Educational Purposes.* Committee Print, House Committee on Education and Labor, 87 Cong., 2 sess. Washington, D. C., 1963.

Poore, Ben Perley, ed. *Federal and State Constitutions, Colonial Charters and Other Organic Laws of the United States.* 2 vols. Washington, D. C., 1878.

Quattlebaum, Charles A. *Federal Educational Policies, Programs and Proposals.* Committee Print, 86 Cong., 2 sess., Committee on Education and Labor. Washington, D. C., March 1960.

Shurtleff, Nathaniel B., ed. *Records of the Governor and Company of the Massachusetts Bay in New England, 1628–1686.* 6 vols. Boston, 1853.

U. S., Bureau of Land Management. *Public Land Statistics, 1963.* Washington, D. C., 1963.

———. *Public Land Statistics, 1965.* Washington, D. C., 1965.

U. S., Congress. *American State Papers. Documents, Legislative and Executive, of the Congress of the United States.* Misc. vol. 1. Washington, D. C., 1834.

———. *Annals of the Congress of the United States: The Debates and Proceedings in the Congress of the United States, 1789–1824.* 42 vols. Washington, D. C., 1834–1856.

———. *Congressional Debates: Register of Debates in Congress, 1824–1837.* 29 vols. Washington, D. C., 1825–1837.

———. *The Congressional Globe: Containing the Debates and Proceedings, 1833–1873.* 109 vols. Washington, D. C., 1834–1873.

———. *Congressional Record: Containing the Proceedings and Debates, 1873–.* Washington, D. C., 1873–1967.

———. *Journals of the American Congress, 1774–1788.* 4 vols. Washington, D. C., 1823.

———. *Statutes at Large of the United States of America, 1789–.* Boston and Washington, D. C.

U. S., Congress, House. *House Documents.* 59 Cong., 2 sess., vol. 91, pt. 2. Washington, D. C., 1909.

————. *Journal of the House of Representatives of the United States.* Annual volumes since 1789. Washington, D. C., and Philadelphia.

————. "Report of the United States Public Lands Commissioner, 1880," *House Executive Document 47.* 46 Cong., 3 sess., vol. 25, pt. 4.

U. S., Congress, Senate. *Journal of the Senate of the United States.* Annual volumes since 1789. Washington, D. C., and Philadelphia.

U. S., Department of the Interior, Bureau of Education. *Agricultural and Mechanical Colleges. Bulletin No. 8.* Washington, D. C., 1920.

————. *Federal Laws and Rulings Relating to Morrill and Supplementary Morrill Funds for Land-Grant Colleges and Universities. Pamphlet No. 91.* Washington, D. C., 1940.

U. S., General Land Office. *School Lands—Land Grants to States and Territories for Educational Purposes. Information Bulletin No. 1.* Washington, D. C., 1939.

BOOKS

Adams, Charles K. *Washington and Higher Education.* Ithaca, N. Y., 1888.

Allen, Hollis P. *The Federal Government and Education.* New York, 1950.

Axt, Richard G. *The Federal Government and Financing Higher Education.* New York, 1952.

Babbidge, Homer D., and Rosenzweig, Robert H. *The Federal Interest in Higher Education.* New York, 1962.

Bailyn, Bernard. *Education in the Forming of American Society.* Chapel Hill, 1960.

Bancroft, George. *History of the Formation of the Constitution of the United States of America.* 2 vols. New York, 1884.

Barnard, Henry, ed. *American Journal of Education*. 14 vols. London, 1855–1866.

Becker, Carl L. *Cornell University: Founders and Founding*. Ithaca, N. Y., 1943.

Bell, Sadie. *The Church, the State, and Education in Virginia*. New York, 1930.

Blackmar, Frank W. *The History of Federal and State Aid to Higher Education in the United States*. Washington, D. C., 1890.

Brody, Alexander. *The American State and Higher Education: The Legal, Political, and Constitutional Relationships*. Washington, D. C., 1935.

Bronson, Walter C. *The History of Brown University, 1764–1914*. Providence, 1914.

Brubacher, John S., and Rudy, Willis. *Higher Education in Transition*. New York, 1958.

Bush, George Gary. *History of Higher Education in Massachusetts*. Washington, D. C., 1891.

Butts, Freeman R., and Cremin, Lawrence A. *A History of Education in American Culture*. New York, 1953.

Carlton, Frank Tracy. *Economic Influences upon Educational Progress in the United States, 1820–1850*. Bulletin of the University of Wisconsin 221. Madison, 1908.

Carriel, Mary. *The Life of Jonathan Baldwin Turner*. Urbana, Ill., 1961.

Carstensen, Vernon. *The Public Lands*. Madison, Wis., 1963.

Cheyney, Edward Potts. *History of the University of Pennsylvania, 1740–1940*. Philadelphia, 1940.

Clawson, Marion, and Held, Burnett. *Federal Lands: Their Use and Management*. Baltimore, 1957.

Clews, Elsie W. *Educational Legislation and Administration of the Colonial Governments*. New York, 1899.

Commager, Henry Steele. *Meet the U.S.A.* New York, 1970.

Crane, Theodore Rawson. *The Colleges and the Public, 1787–1862*. New York, 1962.

Cubberley, Ellwood P. *Public Education in the United States*. Boston, 1934.

Curoe, Philip R. V. *Educational Attitudes and Policies of Organized Labor in the United States.* New York, 1926.

Curti, Merle. *The Social Ideas of American Educators.* New York, 1959.

————, and Carstensen, Vernon. *The University of Wisconsin.* 2 vols. Madison, 1949.

Cutler, William Parker, and Cutler, Julia Perkins. *Life, Journals, and Correspondence of Reverend Manasseh Cutler.* 2 vols. Cincinnati, 1888.

Demarest, William H. S. *A History of Rutgers College, 1766–1924.* New Brunswick, N. J., 1924.

Dexter, Franklin B., ed. *Documentary History of Yale University, 1701–1745.* New Haven, 1916.

Dobbins, Charles, ed. *Higher Education and the Federal Government.* Washington, D. C., 1963.

Donaldson, Thomas Corwin. *The Public Domain.* Washington, D. C., 1884.

Dupree, A. Hunter. *Science in the Federal Government.* New York, 1957.

Eblen, Jack Ericson. *The First and Second United States Empires.* Pittsburgh, 1968.

Eddy, Edward Danforth, Jr. *Colleges for our Land and Time: The Land-Grant Idea in American Education.* New York, 1956.

Farrand, Max, ed. *Records of the Federal Convention of 1787.* 4 vols. New Haven, 1911–1937.

Ford, Amelia Clewley. *Colonial Precedents of our National Land System as it existed in 1800.* Bulletin of the University of Wisconsin 352. Madison, 1910.

Foster, Margery S. *"Out of Smalle Beginings . . ." An Economic History of Harvard College in the Puritan Period, 1636–1712.* Cambridge, Mass., 1962.

Gates, Paul Wallace. *The Farmers' Age: Agriculture 1815–1860.* New York, 1960.

————. *The Wisconsin Pine Lands of Cornell University.* Ithaca, N. Y., 1943.

Gilpin, Henry D., ed. *The Papers of James Madison*. 3 vols. Washington, D. C., 1840.

Guild, Reuben A. *An Early History of Brown University*. Providence, 1897.

Hansen, Allen O. *Liberalism and American Education in the Eighteenth Century*. New York, 1926.

Hart, Albert Bushnell. *Documents Illustrating State Land Claims and Cessions, 1776–1802*. New York, 1895.

Haskins, George Lee. *Law and Authority in Early Massachusetts*. New York, 1960.

Hartwell, Henry, Blair, James, and Chilton, Edward, eds. *The Present State of Virginia and the College*. Williamsburg, Va., 1940.

Hibbard, Benjamin Horace. *A History of the Public Land Policies*. New York, 1939.

A History of Columbia University, 1754–1904. New York, 1904.

Honeywell, Roy. *The Educational Work of Thomas Jefferson*. Cambridge, Mass., 1931.

Jones, C. R., ed. *Report of the Committee on Engineering Extension Stations*. Association of Land-Grant Colleges and Universities Reports. Lancaster, Pa., 1923.

Key, V. O., Jr. *The Administration of Federal Grants to the States*. Chicago, 1937.

Kidd, Charles V. *American Universities and Federal Research*. Cambridge, Mass., 1959.

Knight, Douglas M., ed. *The Federal Government and Higher Education*. Englewood Cliffs, N. J., 1960.

Labaree, Leonard W., ed. *Royal Instructions to British Colonial Governors, 1670–1776*. 2 vols. New York, 1935.

Lee, Gordon Canfield. *The Struggle for Federal Aid, First Phase*. New York, 1949.

Madsen, David. *The National University—Enduring Dream of the U. S.* Detroit, 1966.

March, Paul. *Federal Aid to Science Education*. Syracuse, N. Y., 1963.

Morison, Samuel E. *The Founding of Harvard College*. Cambridge, Mass., 1935.

————. *Harvard College in the 17th Century*. 2 vols. Cambridge, Mass., 1936.

Morrill, Justin. *Address* (1887). Reprinted under the title, *I Would Have Higher Education more widely Disseminated*. Amherst, Mass., 1961.

Mullinger, James Bass. *The University of Cambridge*. 3 vols. Cambridge, England, 1873–1911.

Mumford, F. B. *The Land-Grant College Movement*, Columbia, Mo., 1940.

Munger, Frank J., and Fenno, Richard F., Jr. *National Politics and Federal Aid to Education*. Syracuse, N. Y., 1962.

Nevins, Allan. *The State Universities and Democracy*. Urbana, Ill., 1962.

Notestein, Wallace. *The English People on the Eve of Colonization, 1603–1630*. New York, 1954.

Orlans, Harold. *The Effects of Federal Programs on Higher Education*. Washington, D. C., 1962.

Oviatt, Edwin. *The Beginnings of Yale, 1701–1726*. New Haven, 1916.

Parker, William Belmont. *The Life and Public Service of Justin Smith Morrill*. New York, 1924.

Peterson, Merrill D. *Thomas Jefferson and the New Nation*. New York, 1970.

Pickering, Octavius. *The Life of Timothy Pickering*. 4 vols. Boston, 1867–1873.

Porter, Kirk H., and Johnson, Donald Bruce, ed. *National Party Platforms, 1840–1964*. Urbana, Ill., 1966.

Reisner, Edward H. *Nationalism and Education Since 1789*. New York, 1922.

Richardson, James D., ed. *A Compilation of the Messages and Papers of the Presidents, 1789–1902*. 11 vols. Washington, D. C., 1910.

Richardson, Leon B. *History of Dartmouth College*. 2 vols. Hanover, N. H., 1932.

Rivlin, Alice M. *The Role of the Federal Government in Financing Higher Education.* Washington, D. C., 1961.

Robbins, Roy M. *Our Landed Heritage: The Public Domain, 1776–1936.* New York, 1950.

Ross, Earle D. *Democracy's College: The Land-Grant Movement in the Formative Stage.* Ames, Iowa, 1942.

Rudolph, Frederick. *The American College and University.* New York, 1962.

Schafer, Joseph. *Origin of the System of Land Grants for Education.* Bulletin of the University of Wisconsin 63. Madison, 1902.

Schmidt, George P. *Princeton and Rutgers.* Princeton, 1964.

Seidner, F. J. *Federal Support for Education.* Washington, D. C., 1959.

Shannon, Fred A. *The Farmers' Last Frontier: Agriculture 1860–1897.* New York, 1945.

Stephenson, George Malcolm. *The Political History of the Public Lands from 1840 to 1862, from Pre-emption to Homestead.* Boston, 1917.

Sudermann, Frederick, ed. *Federal Programs Affecting Higher Education.* Washington, 1962.

Sufrin, Sidney. *Issues in Federal Aid to Education.* Syracuse, N. Y., 1962.

Swisher, Carl Brent. *The Growth of Constitutional Power in the United States.* Chicago, 1946.

Taylor, Howard Cromwell. *The Educational Significance of the Early Federal Land Ordinances.* New York, 1922.

Tewksbury, Donald G. *The Founding of American Colleges and Universities Before the Civil War.* New York, 1932.

Thompson, W. O. *The Influence of the Morrill Act upon American Higher Education.* Burlington, Vt., 1913.

Thwing, Charles F. *A History of Higher Education in America.* New York, 1909.

Tiedt, Sidney W. *The Role of the Federal Government in Education.* New York, 1966.

Treat, Payson Jackson. *The National Land System, 1785–1820.* New York, 1910.

Bibliography

True, Alfred C. *A History of Agricultural Education in the United States, 1785–1925*. Washington, D. C., 1929.

———. *A History of Agricultural Extension Work in the United States, 1785–1923*. Washington, D. C., 1928.

———, and Clark, V. A. *The Agricultural Experiment Stations in the United States*. Washington, D. C., 1900.

Veysey, Lawrence. *The Emergence of the American University*. Chicago, 1965.

Wellington, Raynor G. *The Political and Sectional Influence of the Public Lands, 1828–1842*. New York, 1914.

Welter, Rush. *Popular Education and Democratic Thought in America*. New York, 1962.

Wertenbaker, Thomas J. *Princeton, 1746–1896*. Princeton, 1946.

Wesley, Edgar B. *Proposed: The University of the United States*. Minneapolis, 1936.

Wickersham, James P. *A History of Education in Pennsylvania*. Lancaster, Pa., 1886.

Works, George A., and Morgan, Barton. *The Land-Grant Colleges*. Washington, D. C., 1939.

ARTICLES

Adams, Herbert B. "Maryland's Influence upon Land Cessions to the United States," *Johns Hopkins University Studies in Historical and Political Science*, 3rd ser. (1885):1–54.

Colgrove, Kenneth W. "The Attitude of Congress towards the Pioneers of the West from 1789–1820," *Iowa Journal of History and Politics* 8 (1910):3–129.

Cremin, Lawrence A. "The Recent Development of the History of Education as a Field of Study in the United States," *History of Education Journal* 7 (1955–1956):1–35.

Emerson, Harold L. "Pressures on Higher Education from the Federal Government," *Current Issues in Higher Education*. Washington, D. C., 1965.

Gardner, John W. "National Goals in Education." In U. S. President's Commission on National Goals, *Goals for Americans; Programs for Action in the Sixties*, pp. 81–100. Englewood Cliffs, N. J., 1960.

Gates, Paul Wallace. "Western Opposition to the Agricultural College Act," *Indiana Magazine of History* 38 (1941): 103–36.

Guild, Reuben A. "The First Commencement of Rhode Island College," *Collections of the Rhode Island Historical Society* 7 (1885): 265–98.

James, Edmund J. "The Origin of the Land-Grant Act of 1862 and Some Account of its Author, Jonathan B. Turner," *University of Illinois Studies*, 4, no. 1 (1910).

Kandel, I. L. *Federal Aid for Vocational Education.* Carnegie Foundation for the Advancement of Teaching, *Bulletin No. 10.* New York, 1917.

Kirkpatrick, J. E. "The British College in the American Colonies," *School and Society* 17 (April 28, 1923): 449–54.

Knight, George W. "History and Management of Federal Land Grants for Education in the Northwest Territory," *Papers of the American Historical Association* 1, no. 3 (1886), 79–247.

Kohlmeier, Albert Ludwig. "Federal Aid to Education," *Indiana University Studies* 17 (1930): 8–16.

Land, Robert H. "Henrico and Its College," *William and Mary Quarterly*, 2nd ser., 18 (1938): 453–98.

Le Duc, Thomas. "State Disposal of the Agricultural College Land Scrip," *Agricultural History* 28 (1954): 99–107.

McAnear, Beverly. "College Founding in the American Colonies, 1745–1775," *Mississippi Valley Historical Review* 42 (1955–1956): 24–44.

———. "The Raising of Funds by Colonial Colleges," *Mississippi Valley Historical Review* 38 (1952): 591–612.

Morison, Samuel E. "The History of Universities," *Rice Institute Pamphlets*, 23, no. 4 (Oct. 1936), 211–82.

National Education Association. "The Educational Influence and Results of the Ordinance of 1787." *The Journal of Proceedings and Addresses* (1887), 118–45.

"The Ordinance of 1784 and Jefferson's Services for the Northwest Territory," *Old South Leaflets*, 6, no. 127 (n. d.).

Orfield, Matthias N. "Federal Land Grants to the States, with Special Reference to Minnesota," *The University of Minnesota Studies in the Social Sciences*, No. 2 (March 1915).

Reisner, Edward H. "Antecedents of the Federal Acts Concerning Education," *The Educational Record* 11 (July 1930):196–207.

Sasscer, Harrison, ed. *New Prospects for Achievement.* Washington, D. C., 1964.

Sawyer, William E. "The Evolution of the Morrill Act of 1862." Ph.D. diss., Boston University, 1948.

Shadwell, Lionel Lancelot, ed. *Enactments in Parliament Concerning Oxford and Cambridge.* 4 vols. Oxford, 1912.

Simon, John Y. "The Politics of the Morrill Act," *Agricultural History* 37 (1963):103–11.

Smith, Wilson. "The New Historian of American Education," *Harvard Education Review* 31 (1961):136–43.

"Washington's Words on a National University," *Old South Leaflets*, IV, No. 76 (n. d.).

Wellington, Raynor G. "The Tariff and Public Lands from 1828–1833," American Historical Association, *Annual Report, 1911* 1 (1913):179–85.

INDEX

.

"Act fixing the Military Peace Establishment of the United States" (West Point), 20
Act Providing for Free Homesteads on the Public Lands. *See* Homestead Act
"An Act to Appropriate the Proceeds of the Sales of the Public Lands, and to Grant Certain Pre-emption Rights." *See* Distribution —Pre-emption Act of 1841
"An Act to Regulate the Deposits of the Public Money." *See* Deposit Act of 1836
Adams, Henry Cullen, 123–25
Adams, John Quincy, 21–22, 73
Adams bill, 123–25
Agricultural Division of the General Patent Office, 78–79, 88
agricultural experiment stations, 116–22, 122–23, 125–27
agricultural experiment stations in Europe, 116
agricultural extension, 112, 127–29, 132
agricultural schools, 50, 77, 78, 79, 84, 85
agriculture, aid to, 87, 89, 109–10
agriculture, commissioner of (now secretary of), 121
Agriculture, Department of, 95, 111–12, 117, 121, 126, 128
Agriculture, Department of, Federal Extension Division of, 128
Agriculture and Education, Department of, 79
Agriculture, House Committee on, 85, 98–99, 116, 117, 119, 122, 124
Agriculture and Forestry, Senate Committee on, 118, 124

agriculture, nature of the study of, 115–16
agriculture, secretary of, 121, 124, 128
Alabama, App. B
Alabama, University of, 43–44
Alaska, 50–51, App. B
Alaska Agricultural College and School of Mines, 96 n
American Philosophical Society, 74
Anderson, Richard C., Jr., 57
annual subventions, first, 120
Appropriations Act for the Department of Agriculture, 1907. *See* Nelson Amendment
Arizona, 50, App. B
Arkansas, App. B
Army Plan, 30–34
Articles of Confederation, 29–30

Bank of the United States, 56
Bankhead-Flannagan Act, 129
Bankhead-Jones Act of 1935, 112, 125–26, 129
Barnard, Henry, 74
Benton, Thomas H., 65
Bidwell, John, 99
Blair, Henry W., 107–108
Blair bill, 108, 115
Bland, Theodorick, 31
Brown, Amos, 95
Brown University (College of Rhode Island), 12, 103
Browne, Daniel, 78
Buchanan, James, 88, 90, 105
Burke, Edmund, 79
Butler, Nicholas M., 25

Calhoun, John C., 55, 66–67, 68, 81. *See also* Deposit Act of 1836

Index

DATE DUE

Demco, Inc. 38-293